SAMUEL PALMER: A VISION RECAPTURED

This first edition of SAMUEL PALMER: A VISION RECAPTURED was published as a Commemorative Handbook on the occasion of the Samuel Palmer Exhibition at the Victoria and Albert Museum, London winter 1978–9.

The edition is limited to 3826 copies:

1800 copies numbered 1 to 1800 with five facsimiles of Palmer's etchings.

2000 unnumbered copies with one facsimile of a Palmer etching.

26 copies numbered A to Z reserved for the Trustees of the William Blake Trust, the Victoria and Albert Museum and the Governors of Trianon Press Facsimiles.

The text was composed in Monotype Bembo by The Gresham Press and by Robert Stockwell Ltd., who printed the volume under the supervision of Humphrey Jones. It was bound by J. Muir & Co. Ltd. The volume was designed by Arnold Fawcus and published by Trianon Press Facsimiles 16A St. James's Street, London and 125 Avenue du Maine, 75014 Paris.

No. *735.*

Sunset

Samuel Palmer

A Vision Recaptured: The complete Etchings
and the Paintings for Milton and for Virgil

Published by
Trianon Press Facsimiles
for the William Blake Trust
1978

CONTENTS

The plates reproduced on the following pages were chosen with a view to recalling some of the themes that interested Palmer most and which reappear in his work at different periods of his life. They illustrate, too, the continuity of style and the mastery of technique in his later works, referred to by the authors of the essays in the present volume.

LIST OF PLATES

All the etchings except Plate 6 are reproduced from prints in the Victoria & Albert Museum collection.
All subjects reduced except Plates 12-16 and Plates 20-23

PUBLISHER'S ACKNOWLEDGEMENTS

The present Exhibition at the Victoria and Albert Museum, which is the first major showing of Palmer's work for fifty years, was originally planned on a small scale. But in the event, the enthusiasm of the Trustees of the William Blake Trust and its supporters, and of the Director and staff of the Victoria and Albert Museum, was such that it grew of itself.

This Commemorative Handbook has had an even more fortuitous and spontaneous growth. For any errors and inconsistencies that, alas, there are likely to be, the undersigned is solely responsible.

Both the Exhibition and this Handbook have only been made possible by the goodwill of many friends. I should like to thank warmly all the William Blake Trustees, in particular our Chairman Sir Geoffrey Keynes and Mr. Graham Reynolds, for their special assistance. We are indebted also to the Institute of Traditional Science, whose President, Dr. Haven O'More, is one of our American Associate Trustees, for a generous contribution towards the production cost of the Handbook and the other expenses of the Exhibition. Many friends at the Victoria and Albert Museum have given much thought and time, and I am most grateful to them all, in particular to Mr. Ronald Lightbown, Mr. Anthony Burton, Miss Sue Runyard, Mr. Michael Kauffmann, Miss Tina Huntley, Mr. Ray Smith and to Mr. John Lee, who was helpful far beyond the call of duty with the photographic aspect. I am very greatly indebted for their kindness, patience and encouragement to Mr. Raymond Lister and to his wife Pamela Lister and to my wife Julie, who typed most of the manuscript. Without their help, there would have been no Exhibition or Handbook.

Most of the textual matter and the catalogue material, printed in this Handbook in abridged form, will appear with considerable additional text and illustrations in the forthcoming William Blake Trust publication: *The Complete Etchings of Samuel Palmer and his Illustrations for Virgil and Milton*, on which the Exhibition is based. This volume will contain 112 facsimiles and collotypes, including six hand-coloured plates.

A recently formed non-profit English organization, Trianon Press Facsimiles, is co-sponsoring the present Exhibition with the William Blake Trust and the Victoria and Albert Museum. The principal objective of the new organization is to continue in England the collotype and stencil process that has been used in Paris for making the entire series of William Blake Trust Facsimiles. It will also take care of many of the functions formerly carried out by the Trianon Press, who have been for the past thirty years the Trust's publishers and general agents.

I am much indebted to the small staff, full- and part-time, of these two organizations, Lee Burket, Jasmine Atterbury, Pamela Mendez and Simon Rendall; and to Rosemary Harley and to the printers and binders mentioned in the colophon who have produced this Handbook with miraculous speed.

Arnold Fawcus

FOREWORD

The Library of the Victoria & Albert Museum is delighted to welcome this important Exhibition of Samuel Palmer's later work. It has long been the fashion to undervalue the watercolours and designs of what was seen as a dull Victorian aftermath to the mystical years in Shoreham. The Exhibition, which takes place at a time when there has been a radical revaluation of Victorian art, shows that the visionary mood was never lost to Palmer and that, in those other moods he shared with his age, his work has always its own poetical distinction. We thank the Museums and Private Collectors whose generous loans have made the Exhibition possible. We thank, too, the William Blake Trust for the part it has played in suggesting and organizing the Exhibition, and for their individual contribution to its success Sir Geoffrey Keynes, Mr. Graham Reynolds, Mr. Raymond Lister and Mr. Arnold Fawcus.

Ronald Lightbown

INTRODUCTION

WHILE PALMER was still a youth the originality of his work was recognized by two such different artists as Blake and Linnell. Palmer sold his first painting, one of two landscapes exhibited at the British Institute in 1819, on his fourteenth birthday. Soon afterwards he met the landscape painter, John Linnell, who later, in 1824, introduced him to William Blake.

Linnell, who was to become Palmer's father-in-law, gave the young student much sound advice: to draw from nature, 'to study the figure seriously' and to 'look at Albert Dürer'. His influence on Palmer has, however, been much exaggerated. According to George Richmond, Samuel Palmer's life-long and intimate friend:

> Mr. Linnell owed as much to Mr. Palmer in his art as Mr. Palmer did to Mr. Linnell, perhaps more . . . Mr. Linnell was certainly attracted to him in the first place by the beauty of his work.

However this may be, of Blake's influence on Palmer there can be no doubt. Palmer's admiration both for the man and for his work was unbounded, as we know from the now famous correspondence between Palmer and Blake's biographer, Gilchrist:

> In him you saw at once the Maker, the Inventor; one of the few in any age. . . . He was a man without a mask; his aim single, his path straight-forwards, and his wants few; so he was free, noble, and happy . . .

> Moving apart, in a sphere above the attraction of worldly honours, he did not accept greatness, but confer it. He ennobled poverty, and, by his conversation and the influence of his genius, made two small rooms in Fountain Court more attractive than the threshold of princes [letter of 23 August, 1855].

It was an admiration that was both instant and lasting:

> At my never to be forgotten first interview the copper of the first plate 'Thus did Job continually' was lying on the table . . . How lovely it looked by lamplight . . .

Palmer was then nineteen and he treasured all his life the gift he received at this time from Blake of a sheet of Thornton's *Pastorals* with Blake's signature on the margin,

I

later describing them as 'intense gems of bucolic sentiment . . . utterly unique'. Blake was, of course, sympathetic to Palmer's very unusual and poetic view of nature and he undoubtedly encouraged Palmer to pursue his highly personal style which, during a prolonged stay with his father at Shoreham in the following years, produced some of the most original and loveliest evocations of the English countryside ever painted.

These paintings of Palmer's 'visionary years' at Shoreham have justly received great homage in recent years. It seemed, however, to the Trustees of the William Blake Trust (who some years ago arranged for the publication of a facsimile of Palmer's 1824 sketch-book) that Palmer's later work and in particular his etchings and the related illustrations for Virgil and Milton have been unjustly obscured by the magical works of his earlier period, and that they merited fresh appraisal and fuller recognition. It was therefore decided to prepare a volume dealing in as exhaustive a manner as possible with this less-known aspect of Palmer's work. The Trustees of the William Blake Trust wish to thank Dr. Roy Strong, Director of the Victoria and Albert Museum, and Mr. Ronald Lightbown, Keeper of the Library, who generously agreed to arrange an exhibition of these works so that the public could see the scope and interest of the etchings and paintings that occupied the last twenty-five years of Palmer's life. The Library is the Museum department responsible for collecting fine illustrated books and it is therefore appropriate for an exhibition assembled around Palmer's illustrations to Virgil and Milton to be held in its Gallery. The Trustees of the Blake Trust also wish to express their gratitude to Dr. Michael Kauffmann, Keeper of the Museum's Department of Prints and Drawings, which includes some of Palmer's finest watercolours and mixed-media drawings, and to Raymond Lister who has prepared the catalogue and has assisted in many ways with the planning of the Exhibition. The Trustees are indebted, too, to Mr. Anthony Burton, Assistant Keeper of the Library at the Victoria and Albert Museum, who has, with the Trust's Publisher, Mr. Arnold Fawcus, undertaken the detailed arrangements for the Exhibition.

The Exhibition is principally devoted to Palmer's etchings and to his paintings and illustrations for Milton's *Shorter Poems* and for Virgil's *Eclogues*, both of which are closely related to his etchings. It is completed with a selection of paintings from the Shoreham period and from the later years, which are only indirectly related to the etchings and to the Milton and Virgil series. Also shown are a number of portraits of Palmer and miscellaneous personalia and correspondence related to the subject of the Exhibition. These are only briefly recorded in the present Handbook.

The Exhibition brings together for the first time all these works, many of which have never been seen before in public. It seeks to demonstrate that Palmer's early vision of the

English countryside was recaptured, and that, though he was no longer able to walk in the country with Blake, his imaginative genius had not, even in the last years of his life, been dimmed by Victorian convention against which, like many of his contemporaries, he fought a losing battle.

The Milton Series

Palmer's interest in Milton was lifelong. As a child he was introduced to Milton's poems by his nurse, Mary Ward, who, on her death-bed in 1837, gave him her own copy of Jacob Tonson's edition of Milton's works. Palmer carried this volume with him on many of his sketching expeditions, and there is continual reference to Milton in his letters from 1834 onwards, the last being half a century later in 1881, only a month or two before Palmer died. Palmer's devotion to Milton and to this small volume is attested by his son, A. H. Palmer:

> Years passed by. Years of devoted labour, and of fell temptation to desert the old ideal for a far lower one—years of reading in many books and many poets. Still, my father turned to his old *Milton* with unabated enthusiasm; finding within those shabby covers an universe of delight and (as he afterwards found in Virgil), a vast storehouse of 'imagery and suggestion'.

Again and again in Palmer's later paintings the influence of Milton's works, particularly of 'L'Allegro' and 'Il Penseroso' and of *Paradise Lost*, is evident.

Palmer's paintings illustrating 'Comus' were shown as early as 1855–6 at the Old Water-Colour Society exhibitions but the occasion to start his Milton illustrations for 'L'Allegro' and 'Il Penseroso' was supplied by Leonard Rowe Valpy, Ruskin's solicitor, who had purchased a small painting of Palmer's in 1863. We find in June 1864 Valpy writing to Palmer to ask him if he had anything 'in hand which specially affected his "inner sympathies"'. Palmer replied:

> You read my thoughts! . . . Now only three days have passed since I did begin the meditation of a subject which, for twenty years, has affected my sympathies with sevenfold inwardness; though now, for the first time, I seem to feel in some sort the power of realizing it . . .

> I carried the Minor Poems in my pocket for twenty years, and once went into the country expressly for retirement, while attempting a set of designs for 'L'Allegro' and 'Il Penseroso', not one of which I have painted (!!!), though I have often made and sold other subjects from Milton. But I have often dreamed the daydream of a

3

small-sized set of subjects (not however monotonous in their shape yet still a set; perhaps a dozen or so), half from one and half from the other poem. For I never artistically know "such a sacred and homefelt delight" as when endeavouring in all humility, to realize after a sort of imagery of Milton.

Subsequently Valpy commissioned a series of eight large watercolours to illustrate 'L'Allegro' and 'Il Penseroso'. Palmer went to work with his usual attention to detail, first making a portfolio which his son describes:

> One autumn day in 1864, my father betook himself to the glue-pot, and joined together with a broad strip of canvas two strong mill-boards. Next day this primitive portfolio had fixed upon it a great label bearing the letters 'MIL'.

Palmer made numerous working studies, shown in the Exhibition, which are of beauty and great interest and in their way as fine as many of his earlier 'visionary' works. From this start, Palmer conceived the idea of a series of etchings, illustrating the same passages in Milton:

> The Etching dream came over me in this way. I am making my working sketches a quarter of the size of the drawings, and was surprised and not displeased to notice the variety—the difference of each from all the rest. I saw within, a set of highly finished etchings the size of Turner's *Liber Studiorum*; and as finished as my moonlight with the cypresses; a set making a book—a compact block of work which I would fain hope might live when I am with the fallen leaves [letter 20 October, 1864].

Only two etchings were completed before Palmer's death, 'The Bellman', and 'The Lonely Tower'. Both of these are works of great quality and originality and, though very different, have much of the charm of the more naïve paintings of his youth.

The Virgil Series

Palmer's interest in Virgil was equally great and equally persistent. The influence of Blake's illustrations for Ambrose Philips's 'Imitation of Eclogue I' in Dr. Robert John Thornton's *Pastorals of Virgil* has already been mentioned. Forty-five years after Blake's death, when Palmer had made a translation of the *Eclogues* of Virgil, we find him writing in 1872 to Philip Gilbert Hamerton, whose advice he sought regarding their publication:

> Most likely you are full of engagements when in town, yet I sometimes hope that you will spend a day here in springtime. If you would like to do so as an act of penance, I would annoy you with inquiries as to the best way of disposing of a

completed verse translation of Virgil's *Eclogues* which, right or wrong, I am resolved (all being well) to print. . . .

If Blake were alive and I could afford it, I would ask him to make a head-piece to each bucolic. How exquisitely he would have done it we know, seeing that perhaps the most intense gems of bucolic sentiment in the whole range of art are his little wood-cut illustrations to Phillip's [*sic*] Pastorals in Dr. Thornton's book. They seem to me utterly unique.

Hamerton's advice was that he was more likely to find a publisher if it was accompanied by his own illustrations. Palmer immediately set to work on a series of pen drawings with the intention that they should be reproduced by photo-engraving. There was, however, soon a change of plan and Palmer decided instead to make ten etchings, one for each Eclogue. Palmer had started with great enthusiasm and wrote to Hamerton:

The only way is to aim at no mechanical finish, but to put only touches of love. I hope to make them distinctly the best things I have ever done, and I shall do them with the hope also that they might live after me if all else perished.

In contrast to the Milton designs, many of which were made at Palmer's favourite rural retreats, he was obliged to work on some of the Virgil designs in Margate. By the end of 1879, four of the plates had been bitten and proved; however several of the designs etched, but not bitten, at Margate were abandoned. Since Palmer was at the same time working on the Milton paintings and on 'The Bellman' and on 'The Lonely Tower' etchings, there were inevitable delays and it was not until six months before his death in May 1881 that he was able to proceed in earnest. Only one etching, 'Opening the Fold' was completed to his satisfaction before he died. This was first published by the Fine Arts Society in 1880. Four further plates were left partially finished. However, Palmer had completed designs for the remaining five Eclogues, sometimes making more than one for each. Many of these designs, though never etched, are, like the Milton sepia sketches, of great interest.

Posthumous publication of the Virgil (1883) *and the Milton series (1889) by Palmer's son*

There has been considerable confusion in the intervening years regarding these two series of paintings and designs which so preoccupied Palmer during the last seventeen years of his life. Many were dispersed and have only recently come to light and there remain grave problems that have never been satisfactorily cleared up in connection with

5

the two series which were reproduced and published after Palmer's death under the supervision of his son, A. H. Palmer.

In the case of the Virgil series, A. H. Palmer included the five original etchings, completing the four unfinished plates, and made 'facsimiles' by flat-bed photo-engraving of the designs that had not been etched. The Milton series of large watercolours were reduced and then 'reproduced' by the same process, the very fine 'Bellman' and 'Lonely Tower' etched plates not being considered by A. H. Palmer suitable for use.

It is hoped that in the Exhibition and in the forthcoming Blake Trust publication it will become clear exactly how much in these two important publications was Palmer's work and how his son interpreted what he believed to have been his father's intent.

There is no doubt that A. H. Palmer's own intentions were of the best. His difficulties in arranging for the publication of the two series were considerable. It is to his credit that they saw the light of day at all. Yet until now, these two series have been known mainly through A. H. Palmer's publications. One of the purposes therefore, both of the Exhibition and of the Blake Trust publication is to show for the first time the Milton and Virgil illustrations as Samuel Palmer himself conceived them, together with all the related sketches and paintings.

The Eclogues of Virgil. An English version by Samuel Palmer
with illustrations by the Author, London, 1883

In his preface to the volume, published by Seeley, A. H. Palmer wrote:

The etching illustrating the 7th [*sic*] Eclogue was . . . completely finished by Samuel Palmer himself, and it has been my aim to do as little, rather than as much as possible to the other plates; just as much as would best fulfil what I *knew* to be his intention, conveyed orally, or by the touched proofs and drawings—to do in short, only what was *absolutely* necessary to render his meaning fully evident. Better, some perhaps may say, to have published the unfinished plates just as the artist left them. To this I answer, that by doing so, I should have acted in direct opposition to his last wishes— should have broken the last promise I could make him.

The 'Opening the Fold' etching (which was for the 8th not the 7th Eclogue) was, as A. H. Palmer states, completely finished by his father. The extent of A. H. Palmer's work on the other four is discussed in detail by Raymond Lister in the catalogue section below and need not concern us here. 'The Cypress Grove' plate is signed by Palmer and is considered to have been little touched by his son. The plate of 'The Sepulchre' was bitten a number of times during February and March 1876, and again it seems unlikely (despite what he states, as quoted above) that A. H. Palmer altered the plate very much. A proof, signed by his father, is known to have existed, though it is now untraced. In the case of the other two plates, 'The Homeward Star' and 'Moeris and Galatea', it is clear that A. H. Palmer's work was considerable.

The rest of the designs remained unetched, though there is an early etching for Eclogue 2 'The Rising Moon' published in 1857, which is very similar to Palmer's later design. It is perhaps a pity that A. H. Palmer did not use this copperplate in the volume. Be that as it may, A. H. Palmer decided to make what he called 'facsimiles' of this and of the other unetched designs. However, instead of simply reproducing his father's sketches accurately by either flat-bed photo-engraving or by collotype (both used currently at the time), he determined to interpret his father's intentions and to convert the designs, in the course of the reproduction process, into engravings. As he put it on page xiv of his preface to this volume:

> The other drawings which had not been etched have been produced by that scientific process so characteristic of the present century—photo-engraving. But any mechanical method, however perfect, leaves something to be desired when it deals with work of this unusually subtle nature. *These plates therefore have passed through my hands that they should do the more justice to the originals* [not italicized in original].

It should be explained here that A. H. Palmer used a method employed by many artists, including recently Georges Rouault in his fine *Miserere* series. This process allows the artist, starting from a photographic impression of his design, to re-work and re-engrave the subject as he wishes. In the case of the *Miserere* series, Rouault used every conceivable tool to transform and develop the photographic reproductions of his designs into new and original works of art.

If, however, the artist is no longer alive, as happened in this case, clearly this process is fraught with potential danger. In certain plates, A. H. Palmer's results were not infelicitous, but in others such as 'Pan came, Arcadian tetrarch ever good' (Eclogue 10) the 'facsimile' as printed in the volume seems static and has none of the freedom of Samuel Palmer's design.

The Shorter Poems of John Milton
with twelve illustrations by Samuel Palmer, London, 1889

In this volume, also published by Seeley, A. H. Palmer decided, in our view mistakenly, not to use the magnificent 'Bellman' and 'Lonely Tower' plates. Instead, he adopted the same course as for the Virgil volume, stating in his preface on page xix:

I proposed to embellish an edition of Milton's Minor Poems with reproductions, carefully prepared by my own hand, of ten drawings in Mr. Valpy's collection, besides one or two examples existing elsewhere, and to publish the volume as a companion to the *Virgil* . . . My acquaintance with photography enabled me to try some experiments in certain directions; I was able in time, to overcome the difficulties caused by the strong and photographically rebellious colouring of the originals, *and to prepare the way for the engraving by which I intended to conclude the work* [not italicized in original]. It would be out of place to enter fully into technical matters such as these, and it will suffice to say that, for some time, the progress was slow, difficult, and discouraging.

Without going in detail into the 'technical matters' that A. H. Palmer mentions, it is clear from a comparison of the published plates with the paintings and designs shown in the Exhibition that A. H. Palmer must have spent a great deal of time working both on the positive films used in the classical flat-bed photo-engraving process and on the copperplates themselves. The results, though not unattractive, should not be thought of as Samuel Palmer's work, and it is a pity that the printer reversed 'The Lonely Tower', an error not mentioned by A. H. Palmer in his preface.

The two printed volumes shown in the Exhibition together with Samuel Palmer's original paintings and designs are of considerable technical interest, but it would be unwise to conjecture from these how Samuel Palmer might have completed the two series of etchings had he lived. We know, alas, from A. H. Palmer's correspondence regarding the bonfire he made of his father's sketch-books and papers before emigrating to Vancouver that his views regarding filial protection of a father's reputation were most unorthodox, and seem to us today to be quite unjustifiable.

GEOFFREY KEYNES
ARNOLD FAWCUS

PL. I 'The Brothers in Comus lingering under the Vine'
cat. no. XXV(a)   before 1856

PL. 2 Samuel Palmer. Self-Portrait
cat. no. 28   *c.* 1824

PL. 3 'Cornfield by Moonlight, with the Evening Star'
cat. no. 10   *c.* 1830

PL. 4 Samuel Palmer
at the time he was working on the etchings

Pl. 5 'The Lonely Tower'
cat. no. xxii(a) before 1879

Pl. 6 'The Morning of Life'
cat. no. 10(c)   *c.* 1861

PL. 7 'The Sleeping Shepherd'
cat. no. 6(d)   *c.* 1831

Pl. 8 'Opening the Fold'
cat. no. XI(a)   1880

Pl. 9 'The Bellman'
cat. no. XXI(a)   1879

PL. 10 'The Eastern Gate'
cat. no. XVII(a)   1879

PL. 11 'A Towered City'
cat. no. XIX(a)   *c.* 1868

A VISION RECAPTURED: THE ETCHINGS
AND THE DESIGNS FOR MILTON AND VIRGIL

THE PAINTINGS OF PALMER'S 'VISIONARY' YEARS, a small selection of which are shown in the Exhibition, were done under 'ideal' conditions in the secluded valley of Shoreham, safe from the hated machines of the encroaching industrial revolution (of which Palmer wanted no part). He was surrounded by friends such as Richmond and Calvert—the 'Ancients', as they liked to term themselves, who were all young and idealistic and as yet unencumbered with responsibilities. Here they were visited in a cottage (which Palmer had purchased with a small legacy) by their 'master', William Blake. Here Palmer was able to give full rein to his imagination and to his 'poetic genius', which Blake had taught him must be the inspiration of all 'true Art'.

How different was Palmer's 'sanctum sanctorum', the etching corner at Furze Hill, where he settled almost thirty years later, soon after a series of misfortunes culminating in the loss of his beloved elder son, Thomas More. His son, A. H. Palmer, in *Samuel Palmer, a Memoir*, London, 1882, has given us a description of his 'retreat' at Furze Hill:

> Samuel Palmer's study at Furze Hill was a small, comfortable room, to which only a chosen and privileged few were admitted . . . On one side were other and much larger shelves, holding portfolios, in which were classified the innumerable sketches of all sizes . . . a life's selection from Nature's material, landscape and figure. . . . Then came that *sanctum sanctorum*, the etching corner—a rough, home-made cupboard, standing on a chest of drawers; containing, the one a veteran set of tools and a stock of copper plates, new or in progress; the other . . . some favourite etchings by other hands, and a few relics of the childhood of the son and daughter who were dead . . . a room bare of the smallest pretensions to luxury . . .

Palmer visited Shoreham for the last time just before his marriage in 1837; but the memory of those happy years and of the paintings of his youth which he did there never left him. He was quite unprepared both for the realities of earning a living, and for marriage to the daughter of his early mentor, the painter, John Linnell.

The marriage started propitiously with a combined work-tour and honeymoon in Italy in the company of their life-long friends, the Richmonds; but Palmer, who, in contrast to Richmond, had few social graces and an unconventional style, failed to sell his paintings. However, Hannah, who was a talented artist in her own right, contributed to their expenses by making copies, for a pittance, to please her rather domineering father, whose shadow was never far distant.

After a stay of two years in Italy, the young couple set up house in London. But they were desperately poor. His son in the *Memoir* gives us a glimpse of the lengths to which Palmer went: 'Supposing lessons stop and nothing more is earned, avoid snuff, two candles, sugar in tea, waste of butter and soap. But it is more difficult to get than to save.' To make ends meet, he was forced to give drawing lessons and to accept the charity of his father-in-law with whom he found he had little in common. How utterly different was his married life in Surrey from the visionary days at Shoreham. For Hannah, alas, was no Kate Blake. Where Kate believed in Blake's visions and helped him with every detail of his printing and the colouring of his plates, Hannah spent prolonged periods away, staying with her parents. Her horizons were limited; her conversation and letters related to the nothings of her existence.

Palmer's early paintings, now so much sought after, found no purchasers. For like Blake before him, Palmer was altogether too original an artist for his contemporaries to comprehend. He struggled to maintain his financial independence and his integrity as an artist; but it is not surprising that the quality of his work, although remaining well-executed, fell into a more conventional form.

The loss of his elder son in 1860, following the earlier death of his daughter, were blows from which Palmer found it difficult to recover. He could not bring himself to attend his son's funeral and he never returned to the house where he died. Though Palmer's relationship with his father-in-law had become strained and soured, Linnell, who was a successful and much-appreciated painter, now came to the couple's rescue and settled an income on his daughter which enabled them in 1861 to lease Furze Hill—a suburban house which Palmer disliked, often referring to one of the rooms as 'bronchitis bower'.

But he was now at last again free to paint as he wished and he found in his etchings and in the mixed-media designs required for them a blessed escape from reality and an absorbing challenge that provided a new spiritual illumination and, so to speak, an artistic therapy.

*   *   *

Though Palmer had many endearing qualities, he cannot have been an easy man to live with. His marriage had become a struggle between two incompatible sets of values.

PL. 12 'Sambo Palmer' by George Richmond
cat. no. 29   Sept. 22, 1825 (?9)

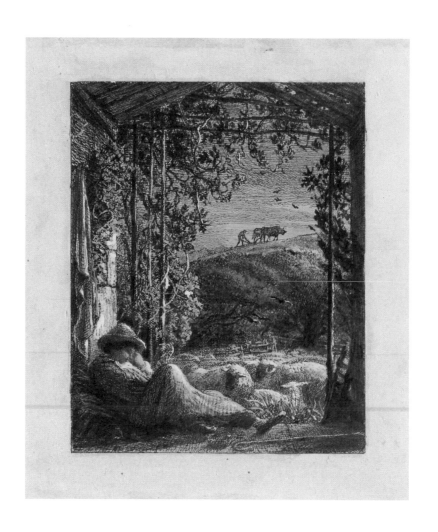

PL. 13 'The Sleeping Shepherd'
cat. no. 6(b)   1857

In an unpublished notebook, now in the Ivimy collection, A. H. Palmer has recorded a much more frank, although perhaps prejudiced picture, of his parents' life at Furze Hill than in the published version of the *Memoir* (part of which was quoted above):

> . . . [My father] saw that the time had come at last when he must have an absolutely inviolate retreat secure from . . . the devastation of his wife's present ideals. So he took drastic action . . . this was the very worst of all the vile painting-rooms in which he had fought his professional campaigns . . . Owing to the fireplace and the bed there was only one possible position for the easel and it was exactly the reverse of what it should have been. One backward step too much, and the painter might . . . sit suddenly on the fire . . . It was a life and a home which would have crippled the artistic efforts of Linnell in an hour . . .
>
> By the time I was ten years old the lives of my parents in a home which one adored and the other loathed had become a compromise . . . On the East side of the door reigned the only conventional member [my mother] of one of the most unconventional and bizarre families which ever existed. On the West side dwelt [my father] the enemy of all conventionality . . .

But all was not discontent and unhappiness. Palmer now set out to finish the translation of Virgil's *Eclogues* which he had started with his son, Thomas More, and later to produce a series of etchings for these. He concurrently began work on designs and etchings for Milton's *Shorter Poems*. And gradually his work became more widely appreciated, and Hannah, too, came to understand him better.

Etching suited Palmer's purpose perfectly since, in his own words, it 'seems to me to stand quite alone among the complete arts in its compatibility with authorship. You are spared the dreadful death-grapple with colour which makes every earnest artist's liver a pathological curiosity'.

Palmer was a meticulous craftsman who found the complexities of etching very much to his taste, and he was able, too, in these and in the preparatory designs to pursue his early preoccupation with the effects of light and shade, particularly in the evening and at dawn. 'The Lonely Tower' and 'The Bellman' sketches and such designs as 'The Brothers in Comus lingering under the Vine' and 'A Towered City' reflect the accumulated visual experience of a lifetime; and they represent a continuity with the style and spirit of his Shoreham work.

The Etchings

But this did not all come to pass at once. He etched his first plate, a conventional little piece, in 1850 and only completed two of his finest plates, 'The Lonely Tower' and the 'Opening the Fold' just before his death.

From his correspondence it can be seen to what extent Palmer entered into the spirit of the etcher's art, dwelling on its physical joys and finding an escape in its difficulties:

> But the great peculiarity of etching seems to be that its difficulties are not such as excite the mind to 'restless ecstacy', but are an elegant mixture of the manual, chemical and calculative, so that its very mishaps and blunders (usually remediable) are a constant amusement. The tickling sometimes amounts to torture, but, on the whole, it raises and keeps alive a speculative curiosity—it has something of the excitement of gambling, without its guilt and its ruin.

Might not etching, in addition, repair his fortunes of which he had long despaired?

> A moderate capitalist might get some picking out of us if he had the wit. Going his rounds he might say to himself, 'There's a promising young man at Red Hill, with remarkably light hair: I'll invest in him.' O! the joy—colours and brushes pitched out of the window; plates the *Liber Studiorum* size got out of the dear, little etching-cupboard where they have long reposed; great needles sharpened three-corner-wise like bayonets; opodeldoc [a Victorian liniment of soap, opium and herbs] rubbed into the forehead to wake the brain up.

This almost hedonistic approach to technique lasted to the end of his life. Every nuance absorbed and interested him, nor was he averse to innovation. 'I was trying, last night', he writes to Richard Redgrave, 'to design something in charcoal with a view to your cherished fixing fluid, and could not help feeling what a difference art etching would be if we could have the variety of point, from sharp to very blunt, which we enjoy in charcoal. Perhaps three or four of the finest etching-needles, or of strong, common needles welded close together, side by side, would do it.'

Every bit of technical information he was able to gather was carefully noted, his son Herbert sometimes acting as *amanuensis*. In one notebook are such details as 'ETCHING Information got by S.P. from Mr. Barlow A.R.A., in Jany 1858 concerning *Etching on Steel*', and sections on drypoint, rebiting copper, transferring a design to copper, printing etchings, copper-plate printing, inks, and so on, the whole occupying many closely-written pages.

Palmer was immensely painstaking, and his progress consequently slow. This is also

22

evident from the fact that in three decades between 1850 and 1880, he produced only thirteen finished etchings. It always took Palmer some time to come to grips with any work and his absorption was often so great that he would spend whole evenings before his easel, forgetful of time, in a silence broken neither by himself nor his wife, holding a candle before a composition to try the effect of light falling on to it from different positions, and absent-mindedly dripping tallow on the carpet. Indeed the full beauty and rich relief of Palmer's etchings can be best appreciated under such conditions.

William Blake, Palmer's mentor and friend, had once written, 'The great and golden rule of art, as well as of life, is this: that the more distinct, sharp and wiry the bounding line, the more perfect the work of art'. Palmer achieved his tone and chiaroscuro by means of lines, sometimes hatched and crossed in a highly complicated web, but far removed from the tones and chiaroscuro of lithography and mezzotint. It was perhaps his love of the linear qualities of etching that made Palmer suspicious of retroussage—the process in the printing of etchings in which muslin is dragged over the surface of the inked plate to pull up the ink in the etched lines and enrich and soften the subsequent impression.

Although Palmer patiently mastered the technique of etching, that of printing from his plates to his satisfaction eluded him. His ideal of what a good impression of an etching should be was summed up in a passage from a letter written on 30 September 1876 to his friend and colleague, the etcher and mezzotinter Thomas Oldham Barlow, R.A.:

> For myself I doubt whether etching in the old sense of the word is not almost superseded by the new art of *retroussage* . . . Sometimes it has been very effective, but, in most instances, is so inferior to linear etching as to become quite another art . . . It seems to me that the charm of etching is the glimmering through of the white paper even in the shadows; so that almost everything either sparkles, or suggests sparkle. Now this is somewhat like the effect of a purely white ground under an oil painting. The *demonstrable* difference may be small, but the real deterioration of a dark ground is universal . . . Well, *retroussage*, if not kept within narrow bounds, extinguishes those thousand little luminous eyes which peer through a finished linear etching, and in those of Claude are moving sunshine upon dew, or dew upon violets in the shade.

He was a perfectionist, and this brought him innumerable torments, as is demonstrated by his detailed notes written on proof after proof, almost amounting to prayers to his trade printers, imploring them to produce the results he desired. An interesting example of this is found on a print of 'The Weary Ploughman':

When the proofs are drawn they should look something like this. The hill behind

23

the farm dark—and the farm not blotty but about this colour—I don't want it darker than this but when the print is drawn wet from the press this would be about the mark. Keep as much ink as you can behind the oxen just under the dog.

Most impressions taken from his plates fell desperately short of Palmer's requirements. He originally installed a small press to enable him to pull his own proofs, but this was unsatisfactory, and he turned for advice to Frederick Goulding, the greatest copper-plate printer of his time. A. H. Palmer, in a letter written on 16 March 1910 told Martin Hardie of the Victoria and Albert Museum the story of his experiences with Goulding, a part of which follows:

> To appreciate Goulding and his workmanship fully, one must have met, what I doubt if you ever encountered, an unfavourable specimen of the species of printer who put the etcher on his mettle (or deep in despondency), by disillusioning him with brutal frankness and in every possible way . . .
>
> There was a courteous and genial kindness of manner; and an evident wish to advance my father's object—the setting up of a private press for our own use, and the thorough grounding of myself in technique. With Goulding's phenomenal intelligence, and his profound and eclectic knowledge of printing, it did not take him many minutes to show me the fallacy of what my father had been joyfully imbibing from Mr. Hamerton as to toy presses with baby leverage—that is for the class of work we wished to turn out. From this cul-de-sac Goulding fetched me with surprising swiftness; and I remember my disappointment at finding that I could not that very day carry home the press under my arm . . .
>
> In due course the press and the rest of the gear were installed at Furze Hill House . . . We soon put aside the two sample plates Goulding had brought down as unnecessary; and got to grips with my father's; that is to say with commonsense, not extravagant 'retroussage'. Here I was able to hold my own; and the proofs we proceeded to pull, turn and turn about, beat any that had been previously produced . . . [on another occasion A. H. Palmer wrote] His teaching had been so absolutely clear all along, so admirably worded, and so kind, that I practically reproduced his proof. This was the foundation laid on which my father at once began to build; the troubles of nearly a quarter of a century were over.

Even so, Palmer was in a state of constant nervous apprehension, for hardly any impression satisfied him. Towards the end of his life he wrote to his son, setting out his view of the ideal conditions in which the printing of etchings should be done, and criticising details of proofs of 'Opening the Fold'. It is interesting to compare his remarks about the use of brown ink with the sepia proof of 'The Morning of Life' in this Exhibition:

24

However much tempests may rage before and after, the Hours of ART-WORK MUST BE QUIET HOURS, and printing like yours *is* art work . . .

Success in the printing of this etching—which printing is your interest as well as mine, depends on delight in solitude and locked doors, a contemplative mood, and intense concentration. Indeed these are the conditions of all high excellence. Men who have these enjoy society all the more by contrast. However much torn by business outside, the great men have been quiet in their studios.

I have just opened the 2 proofs—Pray throw your brown ink into the dust-hole.

I have sometimes thought that, in punishment perhaps for some long forgotten sins—a malignant demon has been suffered to dash the cup from my lip—just when I thought some peculiar benefit had mercifully been sent. Such a demon could have done no worse than to suggest 'brown ink' to you. Both this and the former brown one, are (to adopt a critical phrase of Mr Horsley's) 'BEASTLY' . . .

The Black impression is so very good (the sky absolutely *perfect*) that ten minutes work upon this plate would be enough . . .

The essence of the etching is *crispness*—and anything like the tint left by too thin an ink between the lines, fatal—

Perhaps the dark side of the provender trough is too hard wiped.

I hope you will go over the above carefully as it has cost me my best daylight . . .

When you have availed yourself of the 5 foregoing suggestions it will be sufficient

I think to send me one more proof but no more Browns Oh—no more Browns.

Palmer's greatest dissatisfaction, though, was reserved for commercially-printed etchings like the Etching Club version of 'The Lonely Tower': 'So the dear old Etching Club revives on the 15th—I love it, though it has quite smashed *me*, by the way my Lonely Tower has been printed. Full directions were sent to the printer and a model print but in vain.'

The mixed-media Designs

For almost all the etchings which he completed or planned, Palmer made one or more preliminary pencil, watercolour or mixed-media designs. Though usually freely executed and often very rough, many of these, such as 'The Lonely Tower', 'The Brothers under the Vine' and 'A Towered City' clearly demonstrate that, though there had been a change of emphasis and an evolution of style since his Shoreham days, Palmer had not lost either his inspiration or his mastery of technique.

In this connection it has seemed worthwhile to include some examples from Palmer's correspondence:

Water-colours upon paper hued like the lightest whity-brown paper (I have a sketch-book of whity-brown paper which Mr. Newman got hot-pressed for me: it is very thin however) and with use of white, are most useful for registering passing effects, and soft [coloured] crayons still more so (the *Fixateur Rouget*, sold somewhere in Paris, quite fixes them; even the soft Swiss, which are the best): and they are most valuable, I think, to the *etcher*, by enabling him to desist in a moment from his detailed work, when the right effect presents itself, or the right figures or cattle are passing, and to register those transitory but all-important suggestions in a moment. And in etching at home I don't think a line should be scratched before, at the cost of whatever study, a little sketch is made, showing the general effect (I care not how smudgy), in which the masses and trains of dark are right, and the emphatic lights and darks in their proper places. And this, whether the etching is meant to be worked into tone, or suggested almost by line.

All the kinds of art we are busy with depend, I think, for *their hold upon the eye*, upon the right construction of lights and shadows. I know the vast importance of the above, from having often and shamefully neglected it. Reynolds's BLOT practice from the Flanders and Holland pictures seems to me invaluable. The little effect sketch for the proposed etching may be done best with charcoal, I think, fixing as you get certainties, for you may fix and refix with the *Fixateur* as often as you like.

In December 1873 Palmer wrote to Hamerton again setting out his general views on painting methods. The letter was the basis of an article published in *The Portfolio* in 1876 (pp. 60–4, 90–2). Hamerton wrote: 'he never mixes two pigments if he can get the hue he wants by laying one over another, for superposition being necessarily unequal, there is endless variety of pulsation'. In this letter, Palmer gave a circular schematic diagram, showing the name of a colour in each segment, with a smaller circle, inscribed 'LIGHT' at the centre. This is followed by extensive notes on his methods:

All fading away into darkness, as if in a painted diagram you spread the colour wider and when dry glazed the outer space with black, denser and denser. Then you would understand what brown is, viz. darkened yellow or orange.

We see them thus as they culminate in glory (not in our modern glory of Flake white) and by infinite gradation vanish outwards into darkness. Now suppose you painted another and when dry scumbled it thinly with white, you would have all the generic greys: so then, your greys would have each its prismatic place and name. I doubt whether this arrangement is theoretically perfect, but it answers the end of getting what people call and rightly call the endless variety of 'natures' lines into some order and method—and till the hues are mentally in order, I don't see how we can proceed to approximate or adjust those accidents, the pigments.

For mercy's sake don't quote me! For here is some approach to seriousness, some feeble fumbling after a sort of philosophy, which would bring down a storm of ridicule. How can you proceed a step without Raw Sienna? Why, it is the sheet anchor of tone . . .

You ask whether I think Reynolds's grey ground practice has been at all common since his day—I should think it has been common among the uncommon men who have had correct eyes not only for individual tints but for harmonic influence ruling those tints—as for instance, to mention extremes, the way in which the colours of all objects are influenced by moonlight and by a glowing setting sun.

For precious quality of individual tints we must examine the very early Flemish works, some of them in Tempera, or tempera finished with luxuriant varnish vehicle (by mixing your vehicle with the pigments when you set your palette you command its several proportions for successive paintings from the first deadness to the last glazings)—oil pictures, some of them in a sense, yet so utterly unlike the oil painting of the 17th and 18th centuries that it is a confusion of language to apply the same to them . . .

Samuel Palmer: A Portrait

Samuel Palmer was an individualist and cared little for custom. When he was a small boy his father made him repeat each day the maxim: 'Custom is the plague of wise men, and the idol of fools'. And when he was himself an older man he said, 'If we merely ask ourselves "What will people say of us?" We are rotten at the core'.

Although most of his life fell within the reign of Queen Victoria, he was, in his scorn for convention, one of the least Victorian of men. 'Not once', wrote his son in an unpublished notebook, 'did he resent being regarded as behind the Victorian times. They seemed to him to be times of amazing but disastrous "modern progress" '. Palmer himself often gave utterance to the aphorism, 'The Past for Poets; the Present for Pigs'.

His contempt for fashion found expression in his clothes. As a young man he was something of a dandy, wore white duck trousers and carried a whangee cane, but catching sight of his reflection in a shop window he decided that such elegance did not suit him. He then went to the other extreme, having most of his clothes made by his old nurse, Mary Ward, whose sartorial skill was not her strongest attribute.

His attire included a coat with vast pockets large enough to contain two quarter-imperial palettes with sheets of drawing paper between them, in addition to quantities of books and other drawing materials. In bad weather he wore an all-enveloping cloak and a hat with a brim so large that it also served as an umbrella. He became in short a sight for small boys to jeer at in the streets.

Added to these eccentricities of dress was his decidedly odd build: a powerful trunk supported on unusually short legs—he measured forty inches around the chest, but was only five feet three inches tall. His sight was poor and he found it necessary to wear spectacles which, he said, set 'fair young ladies to think on me, tho it be only to set their pretty mouths a-giggle at the remembrance of my spectacles'.

Despite these oddities he had considerable dignity and commanded respect as soon as he spoke, even though his voice was rather high pitched. He gained respect, too, because he never indulged in eccentricity for effect, saying that it seemed to him that 'nothing is more silly than eccentricity for its own sake'.

He continued to spurn conventions of dress throughout his life, and in his old age even tended (like his contemporary, Philip Henry Gosse, the naturalist) to dress like a parson, wearing a long and loosely-cut broadcloth coat, a double-breasted high-buttoned waistcoat and a white cravat. So clerical was his appearance that he was once asked by a country clergyman if he would assist at a service, and a shopkeeper from whom he bought a hat addressed the parcel to 'The Rev. S. Palmer'.

Palmer went to enormous lengths to patch and repair his clothes, and re-soled worn-out socks by sewing new bottoms to them. And when he felt the cold he was known even to don his wife's flannel petticoat.

In one way he was years ahead of his time, for he was a great washer, taking a tub every day. 'Clean linen only whites the Sepulchre', he wrote, '—clean flesh is a temple for clean and comely thoughts—and it is from the bath or wash tub that cleanliness should radiate through a house.'

In the garden at Furze Hill, where Palmer lived for the last twenty years of his life, he insisted upon having his own inviolate corner in which he could grow wild flowers and weeds, which reminded him, perhaps, of his years of youthful bucolic happiness at Shoreham. Again, as in those years, he continued to enjoy thunderstorms, watching from his suburban garden the effects of lightning and clouds until he was driven indoors by the rain.

There were occasional sorties from his room into other parts of the house as when, with his son, he cleared one of the chimneys by firing a gun up it—doubtless to Hannah's consternation. When he ventured outside the garden it was only for short walks or occasional drives or for attending church, and very rarely for a visit to London.

He could, on such visits, be a somewhat embarrassing companion. In spite of his own

PL. 14 "A Kentish Idyl'
cat. no. 4   1829-30

PL. 15 'Sunshine and Shadow'
An early wash-drawing now
untraced.   *c.* 1829

PL. 16 'Palmer assuming a character' by George Richmond
cat. no. 31   *c.* 1828

peculiar dress he roundly condemned women's fashions if they departed from his idea of the norm, and on a visit to London held forth in his penetrating voice against some hats in a milliner's window, calling them 'Jezebel tops', while a crowd gathered around him and his companion fled.

On the other hand he could be amusing, as when he accompanied himself on the piano while giving an impression of cats singing on the tiles. Moreover he had a keen sense of the ridiculous and loved wit. He was quick, too, to see the pathetic sides of people, though even here his character was contradictory, for he showed little real sympathy or understanding of either of his sons. The elder of them, Thomas More, died in 1861, when he was nineteen, probably as a result of too much concentrated study in which he had been encouraged, even driven, by his father. After his death, Palmer was overcome with remorse from which he never completely recovered.

Yet amid all this oddity and contradiction there lay the character of a true artist, for in his art he had, on the whole, great nobility of soul, compromising and sacrificing nothing that was necessary to it and going to almost incredible lengths to attain his ends. He paid, for example, a visit to London especially to study what he called 'a bit of one inch square, in a single picture'. And, as A. H. Palmer said, 'Instead of settling down to easy subjects and effects, he loved and therefore attempted the most difficult. Constable, wrote Mr Redgrave, painted "under the sun". Palmer carried neutral-tint spectacles, looked the sun in the face and produced such works as 'Evening in Italy', 'The Herdsman's Cottage' and others which included the glory of sunshine transmitted through trees and foreground foliage.' In the evenings he continued the work he had been engaged upon during the day, sitting before a drawing or an etched plate with a candle in his hand, musing and studying effects for hours on end, and perhaps adding a touch, perhaps not, and if he did, perhaps removing it after further consideration.

It is astonishing to note that earlier in his career, in the years following his return from Italy, a strange twist in his character had allowed him to permit his father-in-law to alter or to make additions to his pictures as he saw fit; and again in his later years he consulted Valpy about details of pictures he had commissioned and agreed to change them along the lines Valpy suggested.

To sum up, Samuel Palmer was a most complicated character: a serious thinker hidden under a crust of oddity, a delightful yet irritating companion, a man weighed down by sorrows who could don the motley to amuse his friends. Above all he was an artist whose career was punctuated by two peaks of greatness, the first of which was marked by his Shoreham works, and the second by his etchings and his designs for Milton and Virgil.

RAYMOND LISTER

SAMUEL PALMER, MILTON AND VIRGIL

THE PASTORAL STRAIN established itself early in English poetry. Over four hundred years ago Barnabe Googe was urging the storm-bound shepherd Menalcas to shelter in a cottage where

> Some chestnuts have I there in store
> With cheese and pleasant whey

This invitation in the manner of Virgil's first Eclogue to a wholesome and home-produced meal came some years before Edmund Spenser created Colin Clout, Cuddie and the other true-to-life countrymen of his *Shephearde's Calendar*. From these beginnings the 'oaten stop and pastoral song' did not cease to resound till late in the 19th century. But it took far longer for English painters to follow the example of their poets. It is puzzling that this should be so. In the 17th century, in Italy and France, Claude and Poussin had recreated in their landscape the legend of the Golden Age. Their paintings were the model for the birth of English landscape, but with few exceptions the 18th century pioneers of the form were realistic in their approach to topography. They did not anticipate Archibald Alison's advice to paint 'nature embellished and made sacred by the memory of Theocritus and Virgil'. When Wilson, Gainsborough, Sandby and Wright of Derby adapted the lessons they had learned from Claude and Poussin to the facts of the English countryside they peopled their paintings with contemporary figures, and did not seek to construct scenes in which Corydon or Melibeous would feel at home. The late 18th-century historical painters who chose subjects from the classics preferred those which had figures in significant action, such as Henry Howard's 'Hylas and the Nymphs' from Theocritus; or they dealt in personifications, such as Westall's 'L'Allegro', a very fleshly embodiment of Euphrosyne, the spirit of mirth.

One of the earlier signs of a change of approach came with the foundation, in 1799, of the Sketching Society with the express plan of illustrating 'poetic passages . . . more particularly tending to landscape'. This activity attracted many of the leading artists of the time, such as Girtin, Cotman, Varley and Cristall. They chose the quotations on which they based their sketches from a wide range of descriptive poetry by Virgil,

Milton, Collins, Cowper and many others. Here was a group of people putting into practice the theory expounded by Reynolds in his 13th Discourse: 'A landskip thus conducted under the influence of a poetical mind, will have the same superiority over the more ordinary and common views as Milton's Allegro and Penseroso have over a cold prosaik narration or description'. In their approach they laid the emphasis on the nature surrounding man, rather than its inhabitants. In one of their early meetings they followed Reynolds's hint about Milton, and chose from 'L'Allegro' the lines:

> Towered cities please us then,
> And the busy hum of men

In the drawings by J. S. Cotman and William Havell which have come down to us from this session there is little sign of that busy hum; in each of them a contemplative figure is dwarfed by the cityscape of ruined towers, aqueducts and pyramids which he contemplates.

Work conceived in this spirit, which fitted the current idea of poetic landscape, naturally found a place in the annual exhibitions. Joshua Cristall was notable for the extent to which he exhibited ambitious watercolours illustrating Theocritus, Virgil and Ovid, or more generalized pastoral themes. But it is uncertain whether these compositions had any influence on Samuel Palmer. If he saw them he may well have included them in his condemnation of 'the pseudo-classical, which I hate'. What is unquestionable is the effect upon him of Blake's wood-engravings for Thornton's *Virgil*. Ambrose Philips's 'Imitation of Eclogue I' is not so unworthy of Blake—or Virgil—as his nickname 'Namby-Pamby' might imply. His treatment of the closing lines, in which the older but happier shepherd Thenot invites the younger, unhappy Colinet to stay the night, runs:

> This night thy care with me forget, and fold
> Thy flock with mine, to ward th'injurious cold
> New milk and clouted cream, mild cheese and curd,
> With some remaining fruit of last year's hoard,
> Shall be our evening fare

Blake has entered so thoroughly into the spirit of the paraphrase that his work forms an incantatory evocation of Virgil's pastoral, and reaches beyond it to the less troubled world of Theocritus which preluded it.

In a pastoral landscape which fits the established conventions we recognize that the setting and the figures who people it exist in the past. Blake's wood-engravings are evidently set in an unidentifiable, remote age of genuine simplicity, and are inhabited by figures of venerable antiquity. What gives his cuts even greater distinction is the quality of the light which irradiates the far-off idyllic landscape in which his shepherds work, travel and sing. The rising sun makes the rippling river glimmer; the moon in eclipse picks out the shape of the storm-swept wheat. Or, as Palmer puts it more succinctly, they are 'visions of little dells and nooks and corners of Paradise'.

The study of Palmer's illustrations to Virgil and Milton properly begins with Blake's cuts for Thornton's *Pastorals*. The two signed proof sheets of them which Blake himself had given Palmer hung in his drawing-room, where a maidservant took them to be tailor's patterns. To Palmer they were 'the most intense gems of bucolic sentiment in the whole range of art' and they haunted him all his life. It was their sentiment he emulated when in later life he came to illustrate Milton. Both Blake and Palmer venerated Milton, but their admiration came from different beginnings and was focused on different aspects of Milton's work. Blake came to him in mature life, when 'he was again enlightened with the light he had enjoyed in his youth', and he found in him an embodiment of his own philosophy and, therefore, one of the great exemplars of the human mind. To him *Paradise Lost* offered scope for deeper comment than the early poems.

Palmer, on the other hand, had been steeped in Milton's poetry from his early childhood. His nurse Mary Ward, to whom he owed 'the first moment of poetic impulse' sanctioned this devotion by the gift on her death-bed of her copy of Milton, which he treasured all his life. His designs for 'Comus'—'The Brothers under the Vine', 'The Dell' and 'The Brothers Discover the Palace of Comus'—are amongst the most luxuriant illustrative landscapes he produced in the mid-1850s. So, when Leonard Valpy proposed that Palmer should achieve some heartfelt project for him in his sixtieth year, he could reply that he had carried the Minor Poems in his pocket for twenty years and had often dreamed of a set of subjects from 'L'Allegro' and 'Il Penseroso'.

To the reader of English poetry the earlier verses of Milton are the fitting counterpart to Virgil the pastoral writer. If popular approval is any guide Milton reached the height of his achievement as the poet of country life in 'L'Allegro' and 'Il Penseroso', those cunningly paralleled studies of the humours of Mirth and Melancholy. These two poems compress into concise and pithy images, with a strong visual content, a remarkable range of country scenes and occupations. In 'L'Allegro' the poet is delighted by hounds hunting at daybreak, by watching ploughing, scything, haymaking and the village dance, and rejoices in evenings spent listening to ghost stories and contemplating chivalry, masques and the theatre. In 'Il Penseroso' he identifies himself with the sober-minded scholar who walks at night to hear the nightingale and watch the moon, who pursues his solitary study in a firelit room or lonely tower and dreams away the heat of the day to the murmur of a stream in a shady forest. It is a constant source of surprise to find how much

35

of Milton's phraseology has become proverbial: 'on the light fantastic toe', 'the cynosure of neighbouring eyes', 'linked sweetness long drawn out', 'the cricket on the hearth'. Milton's octosyllabic and end-stopped line has an epigrammatic power, and his concision is carried over into the short titles of Palmer's illustrations: 'The Eastern Gate', 'The Lonely Tower', 'The Waters Murmuring'.

Before he set out to make his designs from these poems Palmer had spent long years in a reverie about them. As well as finding Milton's landscape a constant source of suggestion, he shared another quality with the poet. This was a profound and reflective sensitivity to effects of light in their subtlest variations. Milton links all his country activities with its appropriate time of day, and his two poems are full of minutely observed descriptions of changes of illumination:

> Till the dappled dawn doth rise

> Right against the Eastern gate
> Where the great sun begins his state
> Robed in flames and amber light

> Teach light to counterfeit a gloom

> Storied windows richly dight
> Casting a dim religious light

In the sketch-book he started in 1824 Palmer wrote some lines about twilight:

> And now the trembling light
> Glimmers behind the little hills and corn
> Lingring as loth to part
> . . . the fields and pearled cups of flowers
> Twinkle in the parting light

and his painting is a constant exploration of such effects of sunlight and moonlight. This passion led in its turn to the patronage of Leonard Valpy.

In his chequered career Palmer constantly needed encouragement, and his very help-lessness attracted help from other, stronger characters. These necessary props often became his bane. Or, if he did not complain unduly of their greater resource and strength of character his only surviving son, A. H. Palmer, did with considerable vehemence. Palmer's father, the bookseller Samuel Palmer, was a failure in business and a frequent source of social embarrassment. Yet he gave him the literary foundation which was an abiding stimulus throughout his life. John Linnell was no doubt a domineering and difficult father-in-law; yet his support of Palmer was as heroic and as essential as that he had given to Blake. Valpy is described by A. H. Palmer in unflattering terms. He was, he says, a 'hip and thigh puritan', affected, sardonic, and prone to combine an excessive degree of interference with his help. Yet when we reflect how many plans Palmer drew up for himself and never even started we have to realise how providential it was that he should have had this patron to suggest, cajole and persevere with his requests. He bore with heroic patience Palmer's inborn habit of procrastination; the eight illustrations to Milton which he had commissioned were hardly completed after sixteen years. One of Palmer's countless projects was 'The MONTHS would make a good book of etchings', but even this banal idea was not acted upon. Valpy's persistence ensured his carrying his Milton images nearly to completion. It was a shared interest in light which had drawn the artist and patron together in the first place. Herbert Palmer qualifies his unflattering character of Valpy by admitting that 'he was a man who could revel in the tints of a dying bramble leaf, and who could fling his law and his caution and his seriousness behind him, before a beautiful landscape or a resplendent sunset'. And so the friendship began with Valpy buying a watercolour entitled 'Twilight: the Chapel by the Bridge' from the 'Old' Watercolour Society Winter Exhibition of 1863. He wrote to Palmer to suggest that the light in the chapel was a little too strong, and the artist agreed that the windows 'glare a little and should rather glimmer' and that the proposed modification would enhance poetic mystery. Since Palmer was much put out when his etching 'The Herdsman's Cottage at Sunset' was published with the mistaken title 'Sunrise' it was all the more encouraging for him to have a patron who could enter into the subtle qualities which distinguish one time of day or effect of sunlight or moonlight from another.

Palmer's later technique, both in watercolour and in etching, was founded on the search for ways of rendering these nuances of light. In filling the eye of the spectator with incessantly varied detail he was in consonance with the spirit of his time. The taste of today admires Turner's quasi-abstract 'Colour Beginnings'; but his own patrons were enraptured by such mosaic-patterned watercolours as 'The Blue Rigi' and 'The Red Rigi'. Ruskin justified this pervasive modulation of colour by pointing out that it was founded on Nature, and the truthful artist must copy her: 'It is one of the eternal principles of nature, that she will not have one line or colour, nor one portion or atom of space, without a change in it. There is not one of her shadows, tints or lines that is not in a state of perpetual variation. . . . There is not a leaf in the world which has the same colour visible over its whole surface'. So, in Turner 'every individual stroke of the brush has in itself graduation and degrees of colour'. This exuberance of texture was reflected in most aspects of Victorian life, in the ornate decoration of its architecture, in the multiplicity of objects crammed into its living rooms, in the riot of epithets which gush from Gerard

37

Manley Hopkins's poems, with his 'lush-kept plush capped sloe' and his fondness for everything dappled. Palmer uses every device to enrich his texture in watercolour, stippling, using gum and gouache, scraping out, even applying gold leaf; and he transferred the essentials of that elaboration into his etchings. As he wrote 'it is my misfortune to work slowly, not from any wish to niggle, but because I cannot otherwise get certain shimmerings of light and mysteries of shadow'.

When in 1864 Valpy encouraged Palmer to produce something for him which specially affected his inner sympathies the artist's mind turned immediately to two subjects from 'Il Penseroso'. One of these was 'The Bellman'; the other was to be an indoor subject of similar sentiment, illustrating the lines:

> Where glowing embers through the room
> Teach light to counterfeit a gloom

This, which A. H. Palmer describes as 'an unfortunate composition; sure of being, sooner or later abandoned', was not carried beyond the preliminary sketch, but soon he was discussing with his patron how to extend the series beyond these two subjects.

Ever since Beckford described Alexander Cozens as being 'as full of systems as the universe' English artists have been adept at constructing theoretical frameworks for their range of images. Alexander Cozens's 'Thirty-two Species of Trees', Turner's 'Liber Studiorum' and Constable's 'English Landscape Scenery' are just three of these publications of an analytical nature. Since Palmer was an inveterate system-builder and liked to dabble in algebra as a mental relaxation it was to be expected that he would seek to reveal in his choice of images the comprehensive nature and logical balance of Milton's landscape descriptions. He drew up a table of the leading landscape types and effects in 'L'Allegro', and another showing the parallel or contrasted components in 'Il Penseroso'. Though no doubt he had specific passages for all these examples in mind he only quotes one or two verses from the poems; in most cases he leaves it to Valpy to suggest what passages are most appropriate, and also asks him to say if he has omitted any important categories of landscape described by Milton.

In the course of detailed and intensive discussion the eight subjects were decided. This involved some modification in Palmer's original plan. In the end three subjects came from 'L'Allegro' and five from 'Il Penseroso'; but the set of watercolours divided as he had intended into balanced polarities and holds the scales fairly evenly between mirth and melancholy. What he has done is to compile four pairs of scenes, set successively in the morning, at midday, in the evening and at night. Within each of these four pairs he opposes an optimistic or open sentiment against a solemn or enclosed one. And so the

PL. 17(a) *and* (b) From *Samuel Palmer's Sketch-book 1824*
(pages 27 and 39)

PL. 18 'The Bellman'   ?1864
cat. no. XXI(c)
Probably Palmer's preliminary design,
coloured later, for the etching and for
the large watercolour.

image which Palmer had defined from 'L'Allegro' as 'Sunrise. Fine Morning. Agricultural. Farm sentiment. Hunting. The Pastoral' became 'The Eastern Gate'

> Right against the Eastern Gate
> Where the great sun begins his state

in which indeed the clouds are in 'thousand liveries dight' and

> The ploughman near at hand
> Whistles o'er the furrowed land.

Palmer's watercolour is, in fact, a moorland scene of ploughing on a fine morning. As he says the sun illumines 'nothing but the familiar georgic and pastoral', an occupation fit for kings and heroes. He has included the ploughman and the milkmaid from Milton's text; characteristically the plough is drawn by 'beeves' rather than horses to give a properly old-world atmosphere. To this he opposes from 'Il Penseroso', 'Morning—The Dripping Eaves', also morning, also on the moors, but swept by wind and rain. In this case the beeves are pulling a roller over the newly-turned earth, and he has rendered with minute fidelity the drifting runnels of rain from the eaves. Amongst his comments on this composition are the remarks 'I think wind and wet are a variety worth securing'; 'We may unite the sympathies of poetic remoteness with such homely reality as the smell of newly turned-up earth and the details of a farm afford' and 'I do like the beeves because to me they look ancient and bucolic'.

Midday in a wide landscape is the theme of 'The Prospect', and though Palmer found it difficult to combine the 'mappy Buckinghamshire' lawns and pastures with his Italianate landscape he has conscientiously included them in inconspicuous places where curiosity will in due course discover them. To this he contrasts the seclusion of 'The Waters Murmuring', in which the poet hides from the midday heat 'in close covert by some brook'. Taking the hint from Milton's description of the poet dreaming in this shade, Palmer has introduced the dancing girl with cymbals; 'the nymphs sent by the genius of the wood have just given a staccato tang'. The design embodies for him 'The inland sentiment. Deeply recessed. Cavern; waters falling', and he has sought for 'As much seclusion and enclosure among the mountain clefts as could be consistent with the "pleasures" of melancholy'.

His third pair are evening scenes: 'A Towered City' or 'The Haunted Stream' paralleled by 'The Curfew' or 'The Wide Water'd Shore'. In each of these designs the emphasis is on the water reflecting the sky; in the former 'all depends on the silver stream reflecting the upper sky' its surface broken by the ripples of the waterfall, in the latter he aims at a wide expanse of blank water. In his search for romantic sentiment and

41

remoteness of time and place Palmer has introduced both the 'Knights and Barons bold' and Hymen's 'mask and antique pageantry' in the figures of 'A Towered City'. Palmer refers to this as 'The amber sky', a phrase of Valpy's, and comments that it is 'meant for the quintessence of the remote and romantic in the severe sense of the word. Day rather dreaming than dying'. In 'The Curfew' he makes an effective attempt to suggest the silence of the scene broken by the 'solemn curfew and the lowing steer'.

The final subjects, 'The Bellman' and 'The Lonely Tower' are both set at night. This is the only pair in which both themes are taken from 'Il Penseroso'; indeed either seems to fit his original plan for an image of 'mysterious suggestion. More than meets the eye. The sleeping fold a sort of comfort'. Palmer links 'The Lonely Tower' firmly with Milton's verses by faithfully including in his sky the constellation of Ursa Major, or the Bear, which even unskilled star watchers can recognize because it includes the Plough. In it he aims to reach 'poetic loneliness—not the loneliness of the desert, but a secluded spot in a genial pastoral country, enriched also by antique relics, such as those so-called Druidic stones'. In describing how in 'The Bellman' he is aiming at seclusion without desolateness he remarks 'Increasing gloom sometimes enforces the sentiment of exuberance by giving more play to the imagination'.

The richness of imagery in the eight Miltonic designs have given rise to many profound speculations about their symbolism. But even without recourse to these analytical methods we can see from Palmer's own system how full and how explicit is their content. They are Palmer's survey of the varieties of English landscape and atmospheric effect, so far as they can be related to the descriptions in 'L'Allegro' and 'Il Penseroso'. They are also his imaginative recreations, his memory refreshed from his earlier sketches from nature, of the landscapes which had had most emotional appeal for him. This is not only true of 'The Bellman' with its 'breaking out of village-fever' in its nostalgic return to his Shoreham days. 'The Eastern Gate' and 'The Dripping Eaves' embody the enthusiasm of his sketching tours in Devon and Cornwall; the mountainous vistas in 'The Lonely Tower' and 'The Prospect' hark back to his studies in the Apennines. It was Palmer's remarkable feat to combine the task of illustrating Milton with his personal interpretation of landscape, and yet to cast over all his designs the other-worldly feeling of the antique pastoral.

It is notable that the only two etchings which Palmer managed to complete from these watercolours were the night scenes, 'The Bellman' and 'The Lonely Tower'. He was himself a nocturnal animal, with habits in tune with those of the student in 'Il Penseroso'. In his Shoreham days it was the practice of 'the Ancients' to walk at night to study the moon and stars, a habit which earned them the name of the 'Extollagers'.

Given the peculiarly dense texture of his style of etching, it was in the shades of darkness that he could make most effective use of 'the thousand little luminous eyes which peer through a finished linear etching'. The proofs would reveal most effectively the half lights and half shades of moonlight when seen in the warm flickering illumination of his single candle. After the watercolours had been shown at his memorial exhibition they dropped out of sight until six of them reappeared in 1976; the two etchings however remained relatively well known and so, as Palmer had hoped, they helped his art to live 'when I am with the fallen leaves'.

The search for the recreation of a past Arcadia is felt even more strongly in Palmer's designs for Virgil's *Eclogues*. Their history begins with the ambitions of Palmer the frustrated literary man, who had composed verses in his early sketch-books and imitated the 17th-century divines in the rather mannered archaism of his early letters. When he made his translation of the *Eclogues* he had no intention of illustrating his text, and he only reluctantly undertook that additional task when he had been persuaded that his version would otherwise be unpublishable. His progress was relatively swift, compared with that for the Milton series. In the last nine years of his life he made designs for fifteen subjects, completed one etching and had at least made a start on four further etchings.

Some of the slow, reflective gestation which might have been bestowed on perfecting the etchings was expended on the text of the translation; A. H. Palmer had to make a fair copy of a manuscript absolutely riddled with corrections. Even so, 'Each of these designs took evening after evening of concentration so great, that even my mother never broke the silence'. It must have been a trying household when the studio was to be found in the family sitting room.

Although Palmer's text is diffuse and somewhat old-fashioned in style it is no bad introduction to the mood of the *Eclogues*. His version of the spartan fare which is to greet the benighted traveller, comparable with the passages already quoted from Googe and Philips is:

> Ripe apples are our supper, cream unstirr'd
> Boil'd chestnuts, plenty of the sweeten'd curd.

Yet his prose description of 'Southern Dartmoor sentiment, where the valleys run with cream and where they clout pilchard pies with clotted cream' is far nearer to the essence of Virgil's

> . . . sunt nobis mitia poma
> castanaea molles et pressi copis lactis.

He had conceived his designs for Milton with the highly-finished watercolours in mind. Those for Virgil were preliminaries for the etchings, and since he left them in so uncomplete a state it is difficult to judge whether in the end he would have worked them into an equal pitch of expressiveness. Certainly, when he transformed the sepia drawing 'Opening the Fold' into the completed plate the added subtlety of tone produced by his etched line intensifies the impact of the dewy dawn and the emotional isolation of the love-sick Damon. Had he been able to bestow on the other drawings those 'tender breathings and blooms which after all are the "seasoning as does it" ' he might well have made the whole set a richly varied commentary on Virgil's text. Judged as it has to be from a series of monochrome designs and from etchings completed by another hand there is some monotony in the types of landscape and effects of light. We are conscious of the influence of the ideas which Palmer had borrowed from earlier works of art; from such examples of Turner's Epic Pastoral as 'The Woman and Tambourine' and 'The Temple of Minerva Medica'. Palmer kept some of Claude's etchings in his 'Curiosity Portfolio' and valued them for revealing 'moving sunlight on dew or dew upon violets in the shade', these too must have influenced his design as well as his detail.

Even so, there is in the set as a whole some reflection of the rich range of Virgil's poetic landscape. There are the open scenes of mountainous pastoral country, such as 'O fortunate old man', 'The Homeward Star' and 'Opening the fold'. With these are contrasted the more enclosed scenes in groves and forests. In his design for the fourth Eclogue on the return of the Golden Age Palmer achieves a close relationship to the text which he translates

> Thy very cradle quickens, osiers loose
> To tendrils turn, with flowery shoots diffuse

His drawing for this image conveys the impression of Nature bursting into renewed life through the invigorating impact of the promised return.

In another of the embowered subject, 'In a deep sleep Silenus there reclined', Palmer has reverted to the luxuriant riot of vegetation which he last attempted nearly thirty years before. Here he parallels the Bacchante-like mood of 'The Vine', the plate he made to illustrate the drinking song in *Antony and Cleopatra* for the Etching Club in 1852. In such ways he preserves in his last designs of the world of gods and shepherds a memory of the enchantment with Nature which he first unfolded when he went to Shoreham to make drawings of the story of Ruth the gleaner.

GRAHAM REYNOLDS

In the following catalogue section, to conform with the forthcoming Blake Trust facsimile publication, the etchings are numbered in arabic 1–10, and the Illustrations for Virgil and Milton in roman. The Related Paintings and Portraits (which do not appear in the Trust volume) are here numbered in arabic italics. In the catalogue the titles of the individual poems from The Shorter Poems of John Milton are given in italics.

PL. 19 'Ruth Returned from Gleaning'
cat. no. **1**   *c.* 1828

PL. 20 'The Willow'
cat. no. 1(b)   1850

PL. 21 'The Skylark'
cat. no. 2(a)   1850

PL. 22 'The Herdsman's Cottage'
cat. no. 3(a)   1850

PL. 23 'Christmas'
cat. no. 4(b)   1850

THE ETCHINGS AND RELATED WORKS

1   THE WILLOW: Etching and related work

    1(a) State 1 (1850). Plate size: 117 x 81 mm.; etched surface: 90 x 67 mm.
    Etched signature in the lower left-hand corner: S. PALMER 1850 ('5' reversed).
    Private collection

    1(b) State 2. As published in *The Life and Letters of Samuel Palmer* by A. H. Palmer (1892).
    Signed in pencil: Samuel Palmer.
    Victoria and Albert Museum (ref. no. E1884-1919)

    1(c) The cancelled plate.
    Victoria and Albert Museum

    1(d) Watercolour, gouache and pencil (before 1850). Size: 368 x 270 mm.
    City of Manchester Art Galleries

This etching was Palmer's probationary plate, on the evidence of which he was, in 1850, elected a member of the 'Old' Etching Club.

    The technique is more conventional than in his subsequent plates. He even ruled some of the lines in the sky at the top of the composition, for which he was admonished by Thomas Creswick, R.A.

    According to his son, A. H. Palmer, it 'was practically copied from a careful watercolour study made from nature', No. 1(d).

2   THE SKYLARK: Etching and related works

    2(a) State 2 (1850). Plate size: 124 x 116 mm; etched surface: 95 x 73 mm.
    Signed in pencil: Samuel Palmer.
    Victoria and Albert Museum (ref. no. 640-1911)

    2(b) State 6. Etched surface increased to 98 x 73 mm.
    Etched signature in left foreground: S. Palmer. Signed in pencil: S. Palmer.
    Victoria and Albert Museum (ref. no. E1885-1919)

2(c) Drawing, pen and ink touched with chinese white (1850).
Sheet size: 181 x 108 mm; design area (to border line and extremities): 89 x 68 mm.
Inscribed in A. H. Palmer's hand: 1st Sketch for Skylark.
The Cleveland Museum of Art (Mr. and Mrs. Lewis B. Williams Collection)

2(d) Sepia drawing (*c.* 1831-2). Original untraced; reproduced by autotype process in
Samuel Palmer a Memoir by A. H. Palmer (facing page 22).
Victoria and Albert Museum Facsimile shown

It appears from the advance shown in 'The Skylark' etching, both in technique and content, that
Palmer had become aware that he had at last found a medium which enabled him to express
some of the intensity he had experienced in his youth. He first used the subject in a little sepia
drawing of *c.* 1831-2 which disappeared many years ago; see No. 2(d).

An impression of 'The Skylark' was exhibited at the Cotswold Gallery, London, in 1927, on
which was written in Palmer's hand: 'To hear the lark begin his flight'. It therefore seems certain
that Palmer's source for the subject was Milton's *L'Allegro* (lines 41-2):

> To hear the Lark begin his flight,
> And singing startle the dull night

3 THE HERDSMAN'S COTTAGE or SUNSET: Etching and related material

3(a) State 2 (1850). Plate size: 124 x 102 mm.
Palmer's initials, SP, are etched in the lower margin below the left-hand corner.
Inscribed: early proof before plate was published.
Victoria and Albert Museum (ref. no. E639-1911)

3(b) *The Portfolio.* An Artistic Periodical. Vol. III. London, Nov. 1872.
The etching was first published in this periodical under the erroneous title 'Sunrise'.
Victoria and Albert Museum

4 CHRISTMAS or FOLDING THE LAST SHEEP: Etching and related book

4(a) State 3 (1850). Plate size: 124 x 102 mm; etched surface: 98 x 81 mm.
Etched signature: S. Palmer.
Inscribed: Proof; signed in pencil: Samuel Palmer.
Victoria and Albert Museum (ref. no. E1887-1919)

4(b) State 4.
Etched in the centre of the lower margin: '*Christmas*' | *From Bampfylde's Sonnet*, and in the
lower margin below the left-hand corner: S. Palmer.
Private collection

4(c) The cancelled plate.
Victoria and Albert Museum

4(d) John Bampfylde, *Sixteen Sonnets*, London: J. Millidge, 1778. *Dyce Collection.*
Victoria and Albert Museum

This etching was based on a sonnet by John Codrington Bampfylde (1754-96):

> Old Christmas comes to close the waned year,
> And aye the shepherd's heart to make right glad;
> Who, when his teeming flocks are homeward had,
> To blazing hearth repairs, and nut-brown beer;

The composition of 'Christmas' recalls several details of the illustration no. XVII of Blake's wood-engravings for Thornton's *Virgil*.

It was on the plate of 'Christmas', under the tuition of the great copperplate printer, Frederick Goulding, that A. H. Palmer, who printed for his father, first practised *retroussage* – bringing or dragging up the ink in the etched lines by the application of a piece of folded muslin, so as to give a richer impression.

5   THE VINE or PLUMPY BACCHUS: Etching and related works

5(a) Trial proof, intermediate state 1 / 2 (1852).
Plate size: 302 x 216 mm; etched surfaces, upper subject: 89 x 127 mm; lower subject: 57 x 110 mm.
Both subjects signed in pencil by Samuel Palmer and inscribed by him: Trial Proof.
In the bottom margin, in his son's handwriting: Trial Proof. Later state [*sic*], when the lower subject had been altered in a Vignette; above this: 44.
Private collection

5(b) State 4 (published state). Etched surface of lower subject increased to 60 x 123 mm.
Printed lettering as follows: [above the upper subject] THE VINE. / SONG IN ANTONY AND CLEOPATRA – ACT 2, SCENE 7. [between the upper and lower subjects] SAMUEL PALMER / COME, THOU MONARCH OF THE VINE, / PLUMPY BACCHUS, WITH PINK EYNE: / IN THY VATS OUR CARES BE DROWN'D; / WITH THY GRAPES OUR HAIRS BE CROWN'D; / CUP US, TILL THE WORLD GO ROUND; / CUP US, TILL THE WORLD GO ROUND! [beneath the lower subject] SAMUEL PALMER
Victoria and Albert Museum (ref. no. E1888-1919)

5(c) *Songs and Ballads of Shakespeare illustrated by the Etching Club*, London: Longman, 1853.
Victoria and Albert Museum (ref. no. E1305/1322-1904)

5(d) As above, but in pink cloth binding.
Private collection

The fourth state was published in *Songs and Ballads of Shakespeare illustrated by the Etching Club*. There were two issues of this publication. The small-paper issue measures 321 x 238 mm; it is bound in gold-blocked pink cloth. The large-paper issue measures 411 x 278 mm. It is bound in gold-tooled red morocco and has a different title-page from that of the other issue, on which the date is given erroneously as MDCCCXLIII.

'The Vine' seems to owe something to the influence of Palmer's friend, Edward Calvert, whose wood-engraving 'The Cyder Feast' contains much of the same hedonistic spirit. Certain details also appear to be related: each has a primitive ladder leaning against a tree, abundance is symbolized in each by overturned baskets of fruit, and the running god in Palmer's etching has something in common with the two main figures in the Calvert work.

6   THE SLEEPING SHEPHERD: Etching and related works

6(a) State 1 (1857). Plate size: 124 x 117 mm; etched surface: 95 x 78 mm.
Signed indistinctly within the plate at the bottom right-hand corner: S. Palmer.
Private collection

6(b) Hand-coloured proof of state 1.
National Gallery, Washington, Lessing J. Rosenwald Collection   Facsimile shown

6(c) State 3. Width of plate reduced to 103 mm.
Victoria and Albert Museum (ref. no. 236)

6(d) Pen and sepia wash-drawing (*c.* 1831). Size: 157 x 188 mm.
Whitworth Art Gallery, University of Manchester

6(e) *Etchings for the Art-Union of London by the Etching Club*, 1857.
Victoria and Albert Museum (ref. no. 3714/3743-1902)

Figures of sleeping shepherds occur in several of Palmer's works, including a tempera and oil panel entitled 'The Sleeping Shepherd', and the sepia drawing, No. 6(d). The subject was probably derived from a Graeco-Roman figure in the British Museum, 'Endymion the Shepherd Boy asleep on Mount Latmos', although at first Palmer mistook the figure for that of Mercury. Another source for the setting was probably Milton's *L'Allegro*. It seems possible that the little book lying beside the shepherd may be a reminder of Palmer's copy of Jacob Tonson's edition of *Milton*, given to him by Mary Ward his beloved old nurse on her death-bed. He said that he carried this in his waistcoat pocket for twenty years.

The hand-coloured proof of state 1, No. 6(b), of the etching is of great interest. In referring to a group of his father's works which included this plate, A. H. Palmer wrote: 'I had a notion that it included a "counter-proof" of The Sleeping Shepherd or The Rising Moon coloured by my father. If such a proof exists it must be valuable'. This, however, is not a 'counter-proof', but the quality of the colouring suggests that it may be the work of Samuel Palmer.

7 THE RISING MOON or AN ENGLISH PASTORAL: Etching

7(a) State 1 (1857). Plate size: 179 x 252 mm; etched surface: 117 x 190 mm.
National Gallery, Washington, Lessing J. Rosenwald Collection   Facsimile shown

7(b) Trial proof, intermediate state 2/3.
The Art Museum, Princeton University

7(c) State 7. Size of the plate is reduced to 146 x 222 mm.
Lettered: *Samuel Palmer* 10.
Victoria and Albert Museum (ref. no. E1889-1919)

'The Rising Moon' is the first of Palmer's larger etchings. Some elements, the pastoral scene and the little village nestling in the valley, recall Shoreham while the cypresses are reminiscent of the Villa d'Este. The figure of the Shepherd is similar to that in Palmer's watercolour, gouache and pen drawing 'Cornfield by Moonlight and Evening Star' (*c.* 1830). Both are shown in the Exhibition. The subject is similar to the illustration done *c.* 1880 for Virgil's Eclogue 2, 'Homeward from labour'd furrows bring the plough', No. IV.

8 THE WEARY PLOUGHMAN or THE HERDSMAN or TARDUS BUBULCUS: Etching and related material

8(a) State 1 (1858). Plate size: 190 x 262 mm; etched surface: 132 x 200 mm.
The Art Museum, Princeton University

8(b) State 7.
Signed in pencil: Samuel Palmer.
Inscribed in pencil in lower left margin: Trial Proof. 2nd state of sky.
Victoria and Albert Museum (ref. no. E1890-1919)

8(c) State 7. With Palmer's hand-written notes, transcribed below.
National Gallery, Washington, Lessing J. Rosenwald Collection   Facsimile shown

8(d) *A Selection of Etchings by the Etching Club, London:* Joseph Cundall, 1865.
Victoria and Albert Museum (ref. no. 3764/3775-1902)

Work on this etching began in May 1858 and occupied Palmer for six weeks. P. and D. Colnaghi and Co. Ltd. once had in their possession an impression of either state 1 or 2 marked '1st proving July 3rd, 1858 No. 6'.

A. H. Palmer claimed that 'The Weary Ploughman' and 'Tardus Bubulcus' were the original names of this work, and that the name 'The Herdsman' was nonsense (Victoria and Albert catalogue, 1926, p. 78). Yet there is evidence that the latter title is applicable. The scene appears to occur in May, for horse-chestnuts are in blossom, and ploughing would have been unlikely at this season. Also, there is no sign of harness, which would hardly have been left behind in a field.

The proof, No. 8(c), is inscribed at great length with Samuel Palmer's instructions and comments as follows:

In the top margin: should Mr. Martin wish to take some sample proofs Mr. Palmer sends this as a / Sample for printing from / when the proofs are drawn they should look something like this / the hill behind the farm dark – and the farm not blotty but / about this colour –

In the left-hand margin: Please take care / of this & let me / have it when done with / Keep as much ink as you / can behind the oxen just / over the dog / The man's stick, however, / should not be blotted out / but be as it is here –

In the right-hand margin: Furze Hill House / Red Hill Surrey [partly erased words originally forming part of inscription in top margin] / [Sketch of hills and moon, marked 'A', 'B' and 'moon'] / under the moon close to the / right of the dark Hill B / is a more distant hill A / just where A touches the / moon it should be a little / lighter. Therefore, when / the plate is wiped & / ready for the press / please to take a piece / of rag quite clean / and wipe that line / very carefully – it is / only a little strip of this / hill $\frac{1}{16}$th of an inch / broad that wants it / as much as I have below / indicated in a faint dotted / line [sketch repeated, but with dotted line] / do not wipe more than the / dotted line indicates.

In the bottom margin: I don't want it darker than this / but when the print is drawn wet from the / press this would be about the mark –

9   THE EARLY PLOUGHMAN or THE MORNING SPREAD UPON THE MOUNTAINS: Etching and related material

9(a) State 1 (before 1861). Plate size: 178 x 251 mm; etched surface: 130 to 131 x 197 mm.
British Museum

9(b) State 4.
Inscribed in pencil by Sir Frank Short: 'Working proof. before addition of the dark tree on the right in published state. Martin Hardie has one earlier and one later working proof F.S. Decr. 1912'.
Victoria and Albert Museum (ref. no. E456-1953)

9(c) State 6.
Inscribed: Finished state. Signed in pencil: Samuel Palmer.
Victoria and Albert Museum (ref. no. E1892-1919)

9(d) The cancelled plate.
Victoria and Albert Museum

9(e) 'Rising with the Lark or Ploughing with Oxen', *c.* 1835-6.
Sepia drawing. Sheet size: 105 to 106 x 62 mm; painted area: 78 x 52 mm.
Squared in pencil. Inscribed in bottom margin (probably in A. H. Palmer's hand): 'Rising with the lark / Ploughing with oxen'.
British Museum (ref. no. 1913-5-28-57)

9(f) Hamerton, *Etching and Etchers*, 1868.
Victoria and Albert Museum

It is possible that the designs of 'The Early Ploughman' and of 'Rising with the Lark' were partly suggested to Palmer by the memory of a picture he had seen and been impressed by in the Pitti Palace at Florence in 1839. The work, a variant of which is in the National Gallery in London, is Titian's 'Madonna and Child with SS. John and Catherine', in the background of which is a figure closely resembling that of Palmer's ploughman. A similar figure, in reverse, appears in Palmer's oil and tempera painting 'The Shearers' (c. 1833-4).

Palmer made studies of a plough drawn by Perugian oxen in 1839 during his visit to Italy. It is probable that he referred to these when composing this drawing and etching.

The figure of the woman in the etching was probably inspired by an antique gem carving. Such carvings had always interested Palmer, but he was particularly attracted by them at about the time when he was working on 'The Early Ploughman'.

This etching and drawing should also be compared with the designs of 'Lycidas', No. XVI, and of 'The Eastern Gate', No. XVII, in the Milton series, with which they have obvious affinities.

A. H. Palmer says that the title 'The Morning spread upon the Mountains' was used when the etching was listed for sale in the 1860s by Mrs. Noseda, 109 Strand, London.

The small sepia sketch, No. 9(e), has been placed here since, despite the title given first, Palmer appears to have used it as a working sketch for this etching rather than for 'Rising with the Lark', No. 2.

10 THE MORNING OF LIFE: Etching

10(a) State 1 (c. 1861). Plate size: 181 x 254 mm; etched surface: 136 x 206 to 208 mm.
Signed within the etching at bottom left-hand corner: S. PALMER.
Ashmolean Museum

10(b) State 2. With comments by Seymour Haden, inscribed as below.
The Art Museum, Princeton University

10(c) State 7. Trial progressive proof before completion of letters. Plate reduced to 146 x 214 mm. Roman numeral IV in lower left-hand margin.
Etched in lower margin: Samuel Palmer.
Inscribed: Coll. F. Goulding. Imp. Trial proof to test colour of ink 1871 [in different hand] To Miss C. M. Pott Jan 1902 [on scrap of paper, glued to print] Yrs Truly S. Palmer.
Victoria and Albert Museum (ref. no. E1941-1919)

10(d) State 7. Sepia proof.
Etched in lower margin: Samuel Palmer The Morning of Life 13.
Inscribed: 2 proofs printed in this manner To my Friend R Dunthorne / F. Goulding Imp.
E. Knollys Facsimile shown

This plate has been variously named at different times 'Hercules and Cacus', 'Sheep-washing', 'A Leafy Dell' and 'The Morning of Life'. Of its original state as 'Hercules and Cacus' (of which no impression is known to have survived), Palmer wrote to P. G. Hamerton: '. . . it was begun years ago to illustrate a classical subject; but finding that I could no-how clip my poodle into lion-shape, I even let the hair grow, and christened him for the Art Union, "The Morning of Life".'

The comments on 10(b) are by Sir Seymour Haden, the distinguished and autocratic surgeon and etcher (1818-1910), who with his brother-in-law, J. McN. Whistler, dominated English etching at this period. Palmer disregarded the comments. It has seemed worthwhile to quote them in full below.

There is much burin work on 'The Morning of Life'. In mentioning this in a letter to Palmer, Seymour Haden stated that not only had he made a great difference in strength between the etched and burin work, but it also led to difficulties in printing, as etched lines required stiffer ink than engraved lines.

The proof No. 10(b) is inscribed as follows in Seymour Haden's hand:

In the top margin: All this dirty portion ought to be pure paper as at (B) with the wire mark visible / in it. As much of this paper may be left as margin as the artist pleases – or as suits the subject.

In the bottom margin to left: As this is in all aspects a bad proof – I take it for making remarks upon / Ink too thin – lines not well filled – consequent want of solidity – colour &c.

In the bottom margin to right: [vertical arrow] This piece of copper over and above what is necessary to the subject / I entirely object to – it defaces the proof – spoils the paper – and / enreases [sic] the labour & difficulty of printing – The great Etchers usually / left about as much copper / round the subject as I have / expressed in the line A. – in / fact they etched up to the edge of the copper *and left [the* del.] *as much of the pure / paper round the proof as they cared to show as margin –* / [The last two sentences are continued up the edge of the right-hand margin and along the edge of the top margin; the last is written upside down.]

In the right-hand margin: ¾ of an inch / top & sides & / 1 in: & ½ at / bottom is the / rule – but / provided the / top & sides / are equal / any quantity / A may be / left at bottom / provided it / is greater.

THE DESIGNS FOR VIRGIL AND MILTON

I ECLOGUE 1 'O FORTUNATE OLD MAN!' *c.* 1880

> Pencil, pen and ink and chinese white. Size: 102 x 152 mm.
> *Private collection*

This work illustrates these lines from *The Eclogues of Virgil. An English Version:*

> O fortunate old man!
> Then these ancestral fields are yours again;

The sunburst over the horizon carries memories of the top subject of 'The Vine', while the trees are treated in a similar manner to those in 'Lycidas' and 'The Lonely Tower' in the Milton series.

Resemblances to Blake's wood-engravings for Thornton's *Virgil* occur in many of the Virgil drawings; in this one the figure can be compared with the left-hand figure in Blake's illustration no. XIV.

II ECLOGUE 1 'KNOWN STREAMS AND SACRED FOUNTAIN-
HEADS' *c.* 1880

Watercolour and gouache. Size: 502 x 699 mm.
City Museums and Art Gallery, Birmingham (ref. no. 279 05)   Reproduction shown

This painting illustrates the lines:

> O fortunate who now at last, among
> Known streams and sacred fountain-heads have found
> A shelter and a shade on your own ground.

It could not unfortunately be shown owing to its delicate condition.

III THE HOMEWARD STAR   Begun *c.* 1880. Completed by A. H. Palmer before 1883

Etching for Eclogue 1.

State 3. Plate size: 131 x 187 mm; etched surface: 100 x 151 mm.
The lettering, which appears in state 2, has been removed. Only twenty impressions were taken. Each bears the Dover's House Press, Campden, stamp – a monogram consisting of the letters DHP, with the D in reverse, and the cross-bar of the H supporting a cross. Printed in 1924, after the steel facing had been removed from the plate. Inscribed in pencil: To V. Reinaker from F. L. Griggs.
Private collection

This work illustrates these lines:

> Ripe apples are our supper, cream unstirr'd,
> Boil'd chestnuts, plenty of the sweeten'd curd:
> See, glimmering in the West, the homeward star;

    The etching is one of four begun by Samuel Palmer and finished after his death by his son, A. H. Palmer. The others are 'The Cypress Grove', 'The Sepulchre' and 'Moeris and Galatea'. A. H. Palmer made the following notes about his part of the work on a copy of a letter from F. L. Griggs to himself, dated 27 May 1921 (in the Victoria and Albert Museum):

I laid all the grounds, first and reworking; bit the plates in; did NOT touch the stopping out; proved the plates; and finally "finished" them. So far as I remember I did most to "Ripe Apples are our supper" ['The Homeward Star'], because of all the *designs* that was the only one which was completely finished. The biting was in accordance with my father's new ideal. The mordant (nitrous and water, of course by weight; not measure) is strong as a very tough ground, which had to stand successive stoppings out and bitings, would bear; and the temperature rather higher than usual . . . It may simplify matters if I say that what I did to the Virgil plates was done chiefly with the graver. [not including reducing with charcoal and oil, and punching up].

This bears out a claim made by Mather in 'Samuel Palmer's Virgil etchings' (p. 257; see Selected Bibliography at end of this volume) that in 'The Homeward Star', 'the upper sky is rather mechanically handled', an effect to be expected when engraved work is added to the more pliant work of etching. Mather further claimed that the apple trees on each side of the composition 'are in Samuel Palmer's best style'. He concluded that the biting of the plate was more than half finished before A. H. Palmer added the sky and deepened the dark passages 'none too successfully'. I agree with this view.

The cancelled copperplate is in the British Museum, to which it was presented in March 1959 by Mr. David Gould. It is stamped on the back with the name of the firm, Hughes and Kimber.

IV ECLOGUE 2 'HOMEWARD FROM LABOUR'D FURROWS' *c.* 1880

Sepia and charcoal. Size: 117 x 178 mm.
National Gallery of Victoria, Melbourne

This work illustrates these lines from *The Eclogues of Virgil. An English Version:*

> But see, the weary-pacing oxen, slow,
> Homeward from labour'd furrows bring the plough

A. H. Palmer stated that this was 'the last finished work of Samuel Palmer' (Victoria and Albert catalogue, 1926, p. 49).

The most striking thing about this drawing is its resemblance to the etching 'The Rising Moon' on which it was almost certainly based, the main difference being the presence of the ploughing team, which is essential to the passage the work illustrates. This is doubtless the reason why the etching itself was not used in the book.

The painting of the sheep recalls those in several Shoreham sepias of *c.* 1831, for example 'The Flock and the Star' (Ashmolean Museum).

V ECLOGUE 3 "TIS GENTLE PHILLIS' *c.* 1880

V(a) 1st Version. Pencil, watercolour, pen and ink, chinese white. Size: 100 x 152 mm.
Private collection

V(b) 2nd Version. Pencil, watercolour, pen and ink, chinese white. Size: 102 x 152 mm.
Private collection

V(c) Final Version. Pencil and watercolour. Size: 119 x 178 mm.
Private collection

V(d) Another Version, possibly the earliest. Black chalk, indian ink, chinese white. Size: 102 x 149 mm.
British Museum (ref. no. 1938-11-12-15; catalogued as 'Landscape with ruin')

This work illustrates these lines from *The Eclogues of Virgil. An English Version:*

> 'Tis gentle Phillis I love best of all,
> For when I left, some tears began to fall;

Four interpretations of the same theme – the parting of Phillis and Menalcas. The final version No. V(c), with its magnificent sky, was the one chosen by A. H. Palmer to include in the book, but the first version, No. V(a), gives a more intimate view of the parting. The version V(d), which may have preceded V(a), has echoes of 'The Lonely Tower', both in the presence of the castle on the hill and in the general composition.

VI ECLOGUE 4 'THY VERY CRADLE QUICKENS' *c.* 1880

Pencil, pen and ink, watercolour. Size: 102 x 152 mm.
Private collection

This work illustrates these lines from *The Eclogues of Virgil. An English Version:*

> Thy very cradle quickens, osiers loose
> To tendrils turn, with flowery shoots diffuse:

This composition has much in common with that of the etching 'The Morning of Life', No. 10, with its haunting grove and stream. The figure in the centre distance seems to echoe that in the watercolour and gouache 'In a Shoreham Garden', shown in the Exhibition, and the woman's figure in the etching 'The Early Ploughman', No. 9. The figure reaching into the heavily-laden apple tree could be a recollection of a similar, though male, figure in the top left-hand section of the second plate of Blake's 'The Ecchoing Green' in *Songs of Innocence.*

VII(a) THE CYPRESS GROVE Begun *c.* 1880. Completed by A. H. Palmer before 1883

Etching for Eclogue 5.

State 2. Plate size: 132 x 187 mm; etched surface: 100 x 151 mm.
Signed in the lower left-hand corner: S. PALMER.
As published in the first (large-paper) edition of *The Eclogues of Virgil. An English Version* by Samuel Palmer, 1883. Without lettering.
Private collection

VII(b) ECLOGUE 5 'UNTIMELY LOST, AND BY A CRUEL DEATH'
c. 1880

Design for etching known as 'The Cypress Grove'. Size: 102 x 152 mm.
Pencil, pen and ink, chinese white.
Private collection

Both etching and design illustrate these lines from *The Eclogues of Virgil. An English Version:*

> Untimely lost, and by a cruel death,
> The Nymphs their Daphnis mourn'd with faltering breath.

57

The etching 'The Cypress Grove', follows the preliminary design very closely. An interesting point in the design, No. VII(b), is the bush at the extreme left which is a Shoreham-like detail, such as appears in the treatment of foliage in, for example, 'A Village Church among trees' and 'A Country Road leading towards a Church', both shown in the Exhibition.

The etching is signed, which must indicate that Palmer brought it quite near to completion. Moreover proofs are said to exist signed by Palmer (Mather, loc. cit.), which are little different from the published state; but the possibility remains that work was done on the plate by A. H. Palmer during his father's lifetime.

In view of the foregoing there is some interest in A. H. Palmer's remarks about 'The Cypress Grove' in his Preface to *The Eclogues of Virgil. An English Version:* 'As examples among others, the laden apple tree in the twilight pastoral ['The Homeward Star'], and the huge cedars [actually Monterey cypresses] overshadowing Daphnis' mourners, may be cited as thoroughly realising the views of this veteran etcher' (p. xiii).

The cancelled copperplate is in the British Museum, to which it was presented in March 1959 by Mr. David Gould. It is stamped on the back with the name of the firm, Hughes and Kimber.

VIII ECLOGUE 6 'IN A DEEP SLEEP SILENUS THERE RECLINED'
c. 1880

Pen and wash. Size: 102 x 152 mm.
Private collection

This work illustrates these lines from *The Eclogues of Virgil. An English Version:*

> ... The young Mnasylus came
> With Chromis to a cave, and chanced to find,
> In a deep sleep Silenus there reclined.

The mood, apparently of wine-heavy slumber, portrayed in this drawing is more typical of the work of Edward Calvert than of Palmer, who here for once departs from the gentle pastoralism of most of the Virgil drawings. It was not used in the published version of the *Eclogues*, probably because its subject was considered out of keeping with the remainder.

IX ECLOGUE 6 '– TILL VESPER BADE THE SWAIN'

IX(a) Preliminary version with marginal notes by Palmer, *c.* 1879.
Pen and ink, touched with white. Size: 86 x 127 mm. Squared in pencil. Inscribed as below.
Carlisle Museum and Art Gallery (ref. no. 125-1949-426)

IX(b) Version reproduced in *The Eclogues of Virgil*, *c.* 1879.
Pen and wash. Size: 102 x 152 mm. Squared in pencil.
National Gallery of Scotland, Edinburgh (ref. no. D5023/32)

IX(c) A similar version, 1879.
Watercolour and gouache. Size: 159 x 240 mm.

Signed and dated lower left-hand corner: SAMUEL PALMER / 1879.
Victoria and Albert Museum (ref. no. P35-1919)

These works illustrate these lines from *The Eclogues of Virgil. An English Version:*

> – till Vesper bade the swain
> Number his flock and stall them from the dew,
> And then from the reluctant skies withdrew.

The Carlisle sketch is clearly a preliminary drawing for the Edinburgh work, and probably also for the projected etching.

The Edinburgh drawing, particularly at the right and in parts of the foreground, has the mottled treatment so often present in works of the Shoreham years. The mood of the work closely resembles that of the etching 'Opening the Fold'. It was done, according to A. H. Palmer, 'Before the introduction of the full scheme of light and shade and the sky, which were to be incorporated from the separate chiaroscuro scheme' (Victoria and Albert catalogue, 1926, p. 50).

The composition of the Victoria and Albert watercolour IX(c) is very similar to that of the drawing IX(a) and (b). This brilliantly coloured work is now known as 'Going to Fold'. According to the Victoria and Albert 1926 exhibition catalogue there was an inscription on the backboard, which is now untraced: 'Western Shores [partially obliterated]; Samuel Palmer Furze Hill House, Mead Vale, Red Hill Surrey' [in faded ink written by the artist].

According to A. H. Palmer the Carlisle design was 'the last unfinished work of S. Palmer' (Victoria and Albert catalogue, 1926, p. 51). It is a working drawing for the scheme of chiaroscuro to be used in the later version.

It is inscribed as follows in the artist's hand:

In the bottom margin, reading vertically from the bottom: black / turning [?] / brown. [Reading horizontally:] Stone well over spouting / Water behind boys head connecting with light / field mass other sheep into half tint.

In the right-hand margin, reading vertically from bottom: Rich dark coming near / 6 by 4 / [illegible] better pro[gression?] if it has less foreground. [Reading horizontally]: Golden light / Tr[iangle?] / of texture / light.

In the top margin: 143.6: 4 5 6 ⌊120/ 3 1/3.

In the left-hand margin reading vertically from bottom: 5 1/3 1/3.

In the left-hand margin reading vertically from top: this is 4 to 2.

There are also other illegible marks and several brackets in the bottom and vertical margins. There are unclear areas throughout the inscription.

The line of figures in the top margin is an algebraic problem:

$$\frac{6}{4} = \frac{5}{X} , \; 6\,x = 20, \; X = 3\tfrac{1}{3},$$ i.e. the proportion 6:4 equals that of 5:3⅓.

In view of this it is interesting to recall Palmer's remarks in a letter written to P. G. Hamerton in 1879: 'I love calculation in the abstract . . . equations having been, off and on, my daily amusement for some time' (*Letters* 1879 (12)).

X ECLOGUE 7 'COME, FAIREST, IF THOU CARE FOR ME AT ALL'
c. 1880

Charcoal, pen and ink, chinese white. Size: 102 x 152 mm.
Inscribed on reverse in pencil in the artist's hand: Mist rising behind shed to ½ way up woman's arm.
Private collection

This work illustrates these lines from *The Eclogues of Virgil. An English Version:*

Come, fairest, if thou care for me at all;
Nor later than the pastured bulls to stall
Wind hitherward along the dewy glade,
Ere yet, afar, the rosy mountains fade.

A. H. Palmer wrote that '. . . the charcoal was added after the original scheme of pen and ink line . . . was given up' (Victoria and Albert catalogue, 1926, p. 51).

Another variant on the 'Sleeping Shepherd' theme, although Corydon is not actually asleep here, but resting somewhat like the figure of Colinet in illustration no. II in Blake's wood-engravings for Thornton's *Virgil*. The sheep nibbling the grass at his side resemble sheep in many works by Blake, such as those at the left of plate I of *Illustrations of the Book of Job* and in illustrations I and II of the Thornton's Virgil series. The distant landscape is a recollection of the Apennines and Campagna.

XI(a) OPENING THE FOLD or EARLY MORNING 1880

Etching for Eclogue 8.

State 3. Plate size: 164 x 231 mm; etched surface: 117 x 175 mm.
Signed in the plate lower left-hand corner: S. PALMER INV & F E C.
There is a remarque (spray of harebells) in the lower left margin.
Inscribed: Roof / Bush down / touching / 3 wiped D [ark?] / dark sheep / r [ight?] / Summit mist.
Victoria and Albert Museum (ref. no. E 1466-1926)

State 4. With remarque and publication line.
Signed in pencil: S. Palmer.
Victoria and Albert Museum (ref. no. E 1896-1919)

State 10. Plate size now reduced: 151 x 214 mm.
With a small engraved triangle below the lower left-hand corner of the border line.
Each impression is initialled in pencil: F.S., F.L.G., M.H.: (the initials of Sir Frank Short, F. L. Griggs and Martin Hardie, the printers of this state).
Printed in 1926, when 50 fine impressions were taken.
Victoria and Albert Museum (ref. no. E 638-1911)

XI(b) ECLOGUE 8 'AND FOLDED FLOCKS WERE LOOSE TO BROWSE ANEW *c.* 1880

Design for the etching known as 'Opening the fold'.
Sepia, with signs of scratching. Size: 114 x 171 mm. Squared in pencil.
Signed, lower left-hand corner: S. PALMER.
W. C. Wilder, Esq.

XI(c) ECLOGUE 8 'AND FOLDED FLOCKS WERE LOOSE TO BROWSE ANEW *c.* 1880

Watercolour. Size: 136 x 209 mm.
Private collection

This is probably identical with the watercolour entitled 'Aurora', which was exhibited in winter 1880 at the Old Water-Colour Society (323) and in 1881 at the Fine Art Society (102a). At the O.W.C.S. it was exhibited with a quotation, which included the above line, from *The Eclogues of Virgil. An English Version.*

These three works illustrate the lines from *The Eclogues of Virgil. An English Version:*

> Scarce with her rosy fingers had the dawn
> From glimmering heaven the veil of night withdrawn,
> And folded flocks were loose to browse anew
> O'er mountain thyme or trefoil wet with dew,
> When leaning sad an olive stem beside,
> These, his last numbers, hapless Damon plied.

A. H. Palmer stated that the bitings on the etching plate 'began on the 16th August 1880 and were eleven in number before the first proof was taken' (Victoria and Albert, 1926, p. 85).

Palmer gave his son instructions of how the publication line in state 4 should be placed: 'I think it *would* be preferable to have publication equidistant between the corners of the Early morning – and not a whit higher than we proposed. [sketch] AB equal to C.D. – I have put the inscription too high. The writing should be very small, else it will take away the *proof look* from the proofs –' (*Letters*, p. 1034).

XII(a) THE SEPULCHRE Begun *c.* 1880. Completed by A. H. Palmer before 1883

Etching for Eclogue 8.

State 2. Plate size: 132 x 187 mm; etched surface: 100 x 151 mm.
With etched verse in the lower margin:

> – *while the troubled moon shrunk in and set,*
> *Th' earth trembled, and the starless heav'n was jet.*

As published in the second (small-paper) edition of *The Eclogues of Virgil. An English Version* by Samuel Palmer, 1883.
Victoria and Albert Museum

XII(b) ECLOGUE 8 'AND WHILE THE TROUBLED MOON SHRUNK IN AND SET' *c.* 1880

Pen, brush and indian ink, black chalk, grey wash. Sheet size: 174 x 255 mm; painted area: 102 x 152 mm.
Design for the etching known as 'The Sepulchre'.
Inscribed as below.
The Art Museum, Princeton University (ref. no. 47-183)

Inscribed on verso in pencil in the artist's hand:

		Since 1st filling in grid –
Feb 14, 76	– Mord.	2 to 1 – 1 hour
Mar 3	– – do.	2 to 1 – 1 hour
Mar 27	–	3 to 1 – 1 hour
Mar 31	–	4 to 1 – 1 hour

Upper right: Allen Hook's vehicle for Watercolours DEXTRINE or roasted starch 23 St Paul's ch yard / Gillet's Gillot's steel pens – engraving pen 389;
Lower left: 8th Ecl. – while the troubled moon . . .

These two works illustrate the following lines from *The Eclogues of Virgil. An English Version:*

> And while the troubled moon shrunk in and set,
> Th' earth trembled, and the starless heaven was jet,
> With such as I am crumbling in my hand,
> Could he the sad and shadowy past command
> At will, and while my senses crept with dread,
> From a deep sepulchre call up the dead.

Mather (loc. cit., p. 261) mentions records of biting on the back of the drawing No. XII(b), now in the Art Museum, Princeton University, on which this etching was based, and writes: 'In short this plate was in hand for biting for over six weeks in February and March of 1876; it had been two hours in a rather strong mordant, and two hours more in an increasingly weak mordant. I think we may assumed that such operations and the lapse of time would ordinarily imply a finished plate . . . It was not issued and sold probably because the artist did not wish to discount his project for an illustrated Virgil.'

Mather also records an impression signed by Palmer, which seems to indicate that he considered the plate to be at least near to completion. Despite this, we have A. H. Palmer's assurance that the plate remained unfinished when his father died (*The Eclogues of Virgil*, pp. xii-xiii).

The cancelled copperplate is in the British Museum, to which it was presented in March 1959 by Mr. David Gould. It is stamped on the back with the name of the firm, Hughes and Kimber.

XIII(a) MOERIS AND GALATEA Begun *c.* 1880. Completed by A. H. Palmer 1883

Etching for Eclogue 9.

State 3. Plate size: 132 x 187 mm; etched surface: 100 x 151 mm.
Inscribed: To Basil and Elizabeth Fairclough from F. L. Griggs.

The lettering, which appears in the early states, has been removed. The number of impressions taken is not recorded, but there were probably only a few. Each bears the Dover's House Press stamp, though in this trial proof it is on the back of the leaf. Printed in 1924, after the steel facing had been removed from the plate.

Private collection

XIII(b) ECLOGUE 9 'THE CREAM-BOWL SET AND IN OUR CAVE RECLINE' *c.* 1880

Black chalk, charcoal, grey, white and yellow wash. Sheet size: 139 x 194 mm; painted area: 102 x 152 mm.
Squared in pencil. Inscribed on reverse in the artist's hand: 1st. design for 9th.
The Art Museum, Princeton University (ref. no. 47-182)

This is the first design for the etching known as 'Moeris and Galatea'.

XIII(c) ECLOGUE 9 'THE CREAM-BOWL SET AND IN OUR CAVE RECLINE' *c.* 1880

Pen and ink over pencil. Size: 102 x 152 mm.
Inscribed as below.
The National Gallery of Canada, Ottawa

This design is squared and, as indicated by the inscription on the verso, was used by Palmer in connection with the biting of the etching plate.

Inscribed on reverse with details of biting the etched plate, in pencil in the artist's hand: Mar 3 1876 – (bad silk) – Mordant 4 to 1 – 1 hour (of course by weight) / Mar 6 — Mord. 4 to 1 – 1½ hour / Mar —— 1 hour / March 16 1876 (bad silk) Mor 4 to 1 – 1 hour / March 24 1876 do ditto 1 hour / March 31 1876 do ditto 30 min. / April 1 1876 do 4 to 1 1 hour / April 26 1876 do 4 to 1 1 hour.
  Silk would have been used in polishing the plate (there is no fluff or nap on silk). Old silk, however, decays rapidly and breaks down, hence the 'bad silk' which may have left threads caught in the etched lines. I am indebted to Mr. David Gould for this information.

These three works illustrate these lines from *The Eclogues of Vergil. An English Version*:

> Then, to our goats at milking-time return
> O'er breezy heather-bells and slopes of vine;
> The cream-bowl set and in our cave recline,
> (Its brows with poplar shaded, watch the West),
> And timely, with the sun, together rest.

The etching is less well executed than the others in the 'Virgil' series, from which it would seem that Palmer's work on it was much less extensive. In his Preface to *The Eclogues of Virgil.* (p. xiii), A. H. Palmer said: 'It was his earnest wish that when a subject had been transferred to copper, the plate should be published, even if incomplete, rather than a reproduction of the finished drawing.' There is little reason to doubt Mather's claim that this etching was taken over by the younger Palmer, after being merely transferred, or drawn on the etching ground, and that the biting was wholly his (see Mather loc. cit., p. 259).

In support of this view, it may be observed that the drawings for this work, in the Art Museum, Princeton University, and in the National Gallery of Canada (see the two entries above) are more delicately executed and more poetically conceived, than the etching.

For details of biting see notes to No. XIII(c).

The cancelled copperplate is in the British Museum, to which it was presented in March 1959 by Mr. David Gould. It has the initials E. H. scratched on the back.

XIV ECLOGUE 10 'PAN CAME, ARCADIAN TETRACH EVER GOOD'
  c. 1880
  Pencil, pen and ink, chinese white. Size: 102 x 152 mm.
  Private collection

This work illustrates these lines from *The Eclogues of Virgil. An English Version*:

> Pan came, Arcadian tetrach ever good;
> I myself saw him, glowing as he stood,
> With wall-wort berries, crimson'd like the West.

This drawing was reproduced in *The Eclogues of Virgil* as well as No. XV(b), which is a slightly different interpretation.

XV(a) ECLOGUE 10 'PAN CAME, ARCADIAN TETRARCH EVER
  GOOD' *c.* 1880 A later interpretation of the subject. First version.
  Ink, pencil, chalk, white wash, heightened with white. Sheet size: 160 x 185 mm; painted area: 102 x 152 mm.
  Inscribed in pencil in the artist's hand, edge of upper right margin: <u>edge of cedar</u>, stag in glen.
  The Art Museum, Princeton University (ref. no. 47-181)

XV(b) ECLOGUE 10 'PAN CAME, ARCADIAN TETRARCH EVER
  GOOD' *c.* 1880 A later interpretation of the same subject. Final version which was reproduced in *The Eclogues of Virgil*.
  Pencil and wash. Size: 121 x 178 mm.
  Inscribed as below.
  Carlisle Museum and Art Gallery (ref. no. 125-1949-427)

Inscribed on the mount by Gordon Bottomley: Tenth Eclogue SAMUEL PALMER / V & A Museum 1926 No. 150 / Probably S. P.'s last drawing but one: / See Preface to Virgil's Eclogues.

On reverse in pencil in large writing, probably Palmer's hand: Other side / PASTED / For des ... y [illegible] / ... when dry, scrape with palette knife.

On reverse in another hand: 2nd design for 10th Eclogue.

XVI LYCIDAS

XVI(a) 1873. Watercolour and gouache. Size: 394 x 584 mm.
Untraced

XVI(b) *c.* 1864. Gouache on thick tinted paper. Size: 105 x 151 mm.
Signed lower left-hand corner in backward-sloping capitals: S. PALMER.
R. Tear, Esq.

This work, XVI(b), is undoubtedly the study for a large watercolour now untraced, which was last recorded at the Royal Academy Winter Exhibition of 1891. It illustrates the lines:

> Together both, ere the high Lawns appear'd
> Under the opening eye-lids of the morn,
> We drove a field, and both together heard
> What time the Gray-fly winds her sultry horn.
>
> *Lycidas*, lines 25-8

Scotch pines like those in this work are found throughout Palmer's *oeuvre* – for example in 'The Flock and the Star' (Ashmolean Museum), 'Evening: a Church among Trees' (Tate Gallery) and in the Virgil designs 'Moeris and Galatea' and 'Opening the Fold'. The cypresses are a memory of Italy.

XVII(a) THE EASTERN GATE May 1879

Sepia wash drawing with chalk. Sheet size: 273 x 381 mm; painted area:
190 x 267 mm.
Squared in pencil. Inscribed as below.
Victoria and Albert Museum (ref. no. E1317-1925)

This is a working drawing for the large Valpy watercolour (No. XVII(b)). It was probably developed from the etching 'The Early Ploughman', also known as 'The Morning spread upon the Mountains' (No. 9). A work entitled 'The Morning spread upon the Mountains' was exhibited at the Royal Academy in 1873 (1296), but it is not certain that it was related either to this work or to the etching.

The subject of ploughing was obviously of considerable symbolic interest to Palmer and to other members of his circle. It appears in Calvert's wood-engraving 'The Ploughman' (1827), in Richmond's sepia monochrome 'The Mantle of Elijah' (1882; Sir Geoffrey Keynes), and in several of Palmer's works from Shoreham onwards. Moreover Richmond (and probably also Palmer) was acquainted with Latimer's 'Sermon on the Plowers', and John Flavell's 'Husbandry Spiritualized' was common reading in the circle.

The somewhat granulated and broken texture of many of the details in the Victoria and Albert sepia sketch – such as the distant sunlit field at the left and the foreground – is a type of treatment used by Palmer during his Shoreham years, as may be seen in parts of 'Ruth returning from Gleaning' (about 1828; Victoria and Albert Museum), the oil and tempera 'Pastoral Scene' of 1835 (Ashmolean Museum) and in the sepia 'A Country Road leading towards a Church' of 1830 (Victoria and Albert Museum).

The cottage in the shadows at the right is reminiscent of 'The Primitive Cottage' of about 1829.

Inscribed in top margin in artist's hand: Pricked for 10½ x 7½ May 1879 / Slant of the / amber in the direction of YY [sketch] / Gradation of amber towards azure to the left / of the purple cloud seemed nearly right.

In right-hand margin: [sketch of nude torso from back] Rocky / character / No. 20 [with arrow pointing to hill.]

In left-hand margin: [arrow] / this topmost / shadow [illegible] / of background / horizontal / [illegible] the / darkest / & so down / in gradation / If the sun / is to radiate / over the hill / [illegible] / do not want) / but it will / [illegible] or / [illegible] / [illegible.]

In bottom margin: Length of L. Studiorum.

In addition to the above inscription, the squares are numbered in pencil from right to left in the bottom margin, 1 to 20, in the right-hand margin from bottom to top, 1 to 13, and in the left-hand margin from bottom to top, 1 to 7.

There is a pencil study of a nude torso in the top right-hand margin, and extensive but rubbed and illegible annotations in the artist's hand in the left-hand margin.

XVII(b) THE EASTERN GATE 1881

Watercolour and gouache on London board (see below), mounted on wood panel.
Size: 495 x 705 mm.
Signed lower left-hand corner: Samuel Palmer.
Inscribed as below.
Private collection

A label pasted on back of panel has the following inscription in the artist's hand:

No 1
The Eastern Gate, from L'Allegro
———

Right against the Eastern gate,
Where the great sun begins his state,
Robed in flames and amber light,
The clouds in thousand liveries dight;
While the ploughman, near at hand,
Whistles o'er the furrowed land,

And the milkmaid singeth blithe,
And the mower whets his scythe,
And every shepherd tells his tale
Under the hawthorn in the dale
                    Samuel Palmer
                    Furze Hill House
                    Mead Vale, Red Hill
                    Surrey.

The modernized quotation is from *L'Allegro* (lines 59-68), which the work illustrates.

The year 1881 is the date given to the work in Christie's catalogue of the sale of 18 June 1892.

Turnbull's extra superfine London drawing boards, on one of which this work is painted, were available in sizes from foolscap to imperial and from 2 sheet to 6 sheet in thickness.

XVIII THE PROSPECT 1881

Watercolour and gouache. Size: 508 x 711 mm.
Untraced

This work illustrates the lines:

Streit mine eye hath caught new pleasures
Whilst the Lantskip round it measures,
Russet Lawns, and Fallows Gray,
Where the nibling flocks do stray,
Mountains on whose barren brest
The labouring clouds do often rest:
Meadows trim with daisies pide,
Shallow Brooks and Rivers wide.
Towers, and Battlements it sees
Boosom'd high in tufted Trees,
Where perhaps som beauty lies,
The Cynosure of neighbouring eyes.
                    L'Allegro, lines 69-80

Elements in the composition of this work are related to similar elements in 'The Lonely Tower' and 'Opening the Fold' (Virgil series). The general layout with a rolling landscape, distant hills and the group of trees at the right have resemblances to the latter; the walled bridge and distant buildings are reminiscent of the former. The trees to the right, like those in 'Lycidas' are of a type found in many of Palmer's works.

The mottled effect present in many works of the Shoreham period, and mentioned under 'The Eastern Gate', seems from the reproduction to be much in evidence on the slopes on the right.

XIX(a) A TOWERED CITY or THE HAUNTED STREAM *c.* 1868

Sepia wash. Sheet size: 260 x 413 mm; painted area: 203 x 283 mm.
Squared in pencil. Inscribed as below.
Victoria and Albert Museum (ref. no. 1318-1925)

Palmer's admiration for Claude is apparent in many of his letters and notes, and in one letter to a pupil, Miss Louisa Twining (*Letters*, p. 718), he advises her to copy prints of Claude's *Liber Veritatis* in the British Museum print room. 'A Towered City' appears to show some characteristics derived from this work. The general view, including the placing of the tree, the bridge and the city is apparently the same view, somewhat idealized, of Tivoli (which Palmer visited in 1838 and 1839) in plates 24, 67 and especially 79 of the *Liber Veritatis*. Further, the group of dancers at the right, shown more clearly in the finished version than in the sepia, is perhaps an echo of similar groups of dancers in several plates of the *Liber*, especially no. 129, 'Landscape with the Adoration of the Golden Calf'. (Cf. *Claude Lorrain: Liber Veritatis* by Michael Kitson, London, 1978.)

Inscribed in top margin in pencil in the artist's hand (much is indistinct): Col[ogne] Earth – try very thin bite underneath – Col[ogne] Earth exactly as dark as streak – or Col[ogne] E[arth] Cr[imson] & white to tint / Broad Light on the tops of things under so light a sky.

In left-hand margin: [Bracket with vertical illegible inscription in two lines] / Now I see it / June 6 6 / [sketch of outline of design marked 1 2 3 from right to left. Section 1 marked:] This very / dark – / not misty / Top of purple cloud] / in the [illegible] / of [illegible] / [bracket] not so dark as / castle hill [bracket.]

In right-hand margin: A to *seem* deeper than / the rock-wood [illegible] / at C – A & B to mass / together – A very flat / [sketch marked A B C; arrow pointing to main design] / [arrow] This is brighter / and of sky / some bits of grey in / B a little lighter / than A & perhaps / a touch or two in / B darker than / anything in A / [sketch] / – tree now lower / than this –.

In bottom margin: [Sketch] Perhaps the [illegible] water larger & purest & lightest of all / [sketch] This end of forground to appear as an emphatic dark outline / from which the water falls into gloom outwards through the mist and yet above all to be very dark – very cool.

The last two lines in the left-hand margin are written upside-down. The last line in the bottom margin, after the word mist, continues vertically into the right-hand margin.

The reference to dark Cologne is to an impermanent colour called Cologne earth or Cassel earth, closely resembling Van Dyke brown.

XIX(b) A TOWERED CITY or THE HAUNTED STREAM 1868

Watercolour and gouache, with thick gum in places. Size: 511 x 708 mm.
Signed bottom left-hand corner: S. PALMER.
Rijksmuseum, Amsterdam

This work illustrates the lines:

> Towred Cities please us then,
> And the busie humm of men,
> Where throngs of Knights and Barons bold,
> In weeds of Peace high triumphs hold,
> With store of Ladies, whose bright eies

Rain influence, and judge the prise
Of Wit, or Arms, while both contend
To win her Grace, whom all commend.
There let *Hymen* oft appear
In Saffron robe, with Taper clear,
And pomp, and feast, and revelry,
With mask, and antique Pageantry,
Such sights as youthfull Poets dream
On Summer eeves by haunted stream.

L'Allegro, lines 117-30

The year is that given to the work in Christie's catalogue of the sale of 18 June 1892.

The group of dancers is closely related to those of the revellers in 'The Dell of Comus' and 'The Brothers discovering the Palace of Comus' and recalls the spirit of pagan abandon present in the top subject of the etching 'The Vine'. The Towered City itself is obviously a recollection of Tivoli which Palmer visited in 1838 and 1839. That part of the composition at the centre left where the bridge and the trees meet recalls somewhat the bridge and trees at the left of the etching of 'The Early Ploughman'.

XX THE CURFEW or THE WIDE WATER'D SHORE 1870

Watercolour and gouache on London board. Size: 500 x 711 mm.
Signed and dated lower left-hand corner: S. PALMER 1870.
Inscribed as below.

Rijksmuseum, Amsterdam

The label for the 1872 Annual International Exhibition is pasted on the back panel of the frame. In addition to the name of the artist and the name and address of the owner (Valpy), it contains the following modernized quotation from *Il Penseroso* (lines 73-7) which the work illustrates:

Oft on a flat of rising ground
I hear the far-off curfew sound
Over some wide water'd shore
Swinging low with sullen roar.

This watercolour shows Palmer's preoccupation with the idea of the tower, which to him might have symbolized spiritual aspiration. The tree types are similar to those in 'The Lonely Tower'; and the handling of some of the foreground foliage at the bottom right-hand side recalls that in early works, such as 'A Country Road leading towards a Church' (1830, Victoria and Albert Museum) and 'A Kentish Idyl' (about 1829-30, Victoria and Albert Museum) both shown in the Exhibition.

Inscribed on reverse, top right; in pencil in the artist's hand: Other side prepared and ready.

At bottom right: The substance of the London Board / so much contributed to the Durability / that it should never be damped behind / to get off [the, del.] some of the papers, / an atrocity I know to have been once / committed with a view to making the / surface perfectly flat!!! SP.

XXI THE BELLMAN: Etching and related works

XXI(a) State 2 (1879). Plate size: 190 x 251 mm; etched surface: 167 x 233 mm.
An inscription in lower right-hand corner of plate has been almost burnished away.
Inscribed in Samuel Palmer's hand: [top right margin] Remember the farther roof [lower left margin] For Touching [lower right margin] 3rd Proving / 1st May 1879.
In another hand in lower margin: II of States / A. 11. The Bellman (Touched with Chinese White / in places).
Dr. B. E. Juel-Jensen

XXI(b) State 4.
Inscribed in lower right-hand corner of plate: S. PALMER. INV. ET. FEC/MEAD. VALE/REDHILL/ 1879.
Signed in pencil: Samuel Palmer.
Inscribed in lower left-hand corner in pencil: A.H.P. Private Press 9.6.79 / Proof before remarque.
Victoria and Albert Museum (ref. no. E1464-1926)

XXI(c) Watercolour drawing, *c.* 1864.
Sheet size: 225 x 317 mm; painted area: 172 x 239 mm.
Signed lower left-hand corner in backward-sloping letters: S. PALMER.
Pencil notes and sketches in artist's hand around edge (see below).
Cecil Higgins Gallery, Bedford (ref. no. P.436/P.193)

XXI(d) Sepia and chalk drawing, *c.* 1864.
Sheet size: 227 x 318 mm; painted area: 170 x 236 mm.
Inscribed as below.
Victoria and Albert Museum (ref. no. E1319-1925)

XXI(e) Watercolour and gouache, 1881.
On London board mounted on wood panel 506 x 705 mm.
The Trustees of the Chatsworth Settlement (Devonshire Collections)

These works illustrate the lines:

> Or the Belmans drousie charm,
> To bless the dores from nightly harm.
> *Il Penseroso*, lines 83-4

'The Bellman' and 'The Lonely Tower' etchings were the first of a planned series of plates illustrating *The Shorter Poems of Milton*, but no further subjects were etched.

Palmer expounded his idea in a letter to L. R. Valpy written on 20 October 1864: 'The Etching dream came over me in this way. I am making my working sketches a quarter the size of the drawings, and was surprised and not displeased to notice the variety – the difference of each from all the rest. I saw within, a set of highly-finished etchings the size of Turner's *Liber Studiorum;*' (for complete passage and further details see pp. 17 and 18).

Palmer refers to the etching in a letter to P. G. Hamerton, written on 4 August 1879: 'I am very glad that you like my Bellman ... It is a breaking out of village-fever long after contact – a dream of that genuine village [Shoreham] where I mused away some of my best years, designing what nobody would care for, and contracting, among good books, a fastidious and unpopular taste.'

A. H. Palmer stated that 'The Bellman plate received thirteen bitings, and the usual thorough stopping out between them. The temperature of the mordant varied from 61° to 85°. After the first biting, the needle work was nearly doubled, and more was added after the second, third and seventh.' (Victoria and Albert catalogue, 1926, p. 83).

In a notebook now in the Ivimy Collection, A. H. Palmer wrote: 'The working proofs of this etching were printed by me at Furze Hill and proofs for sale supplied by me from the press which I operated at Newman St.'

The Cecil Higgins watercolour, No. XXI(c), which is squared, may be the first of the working drawings referred to above, and was perhaps done soon after Palmer received the letter from Valpy of June 1864 asking 'if he had anything in hand which seriously affected his inner thoughts' (see pp. 38-42). It seems likely from an examination of the painting and of the notes in the margin that the colouring may have been added at a later date. The drawing appears to have been used both for the large Valpy watercolour and for the etching. The notes in the margin refer to the two oxen in the foreground (whose positioning was slightly changed in the etching) – 'The ox behind it dark, though against the hedge . . . / Remember the nearest ox to be light.' A calf was also added in the etching.

The Victoria and Albert's design, No. XXI(d), which is also squared, appears to be the final sketch for the chiaroscuro effects of the etching; but here again it was probably also used for making the large Valpy watercolour, No. XXI(e). It does not have the dry branches in the foreground which are in both the Cecil Higgins watercolour and in the etching, but which do not appear in the Valpy painting.

Palmer considered this painting still unfinished just before his death in 1881 (*Letters*, p. 1075). For this reason it was not included in the Fine Art Society memorial exhibition held in the same year. A label for the 1893 Royal Academy exhibition is pasted on the back panel of the frame. It contains the following modernized quotation from *Il Penseroso* (lines 83-4) which the work illustrates:

> And the Bellman's drowsy charm
> To bless the doors from Nightly harm.

No. XXI(c) is inscribed in top margin in the artist's hand: Midd. dist wood is thick gamboge over [illegible] finish with sepia [illegible] Sepia / A to be the same width as B or a very little less – Midd dist wood is thick gamboge over [? bistre].

In right-hand margin: Place on plate / [illegible] / ? / [illegible] / Arch a / little more / to right of / church tower / [scribble] / 19¼ x 6¾ [written vertically] / [sketch of cow] / This the cow [illegible] / light [illegible] / [sketch of ox] / The ox behind it / dark – though against hedge / [sketch of ox.]

In left-hand margin:
1 5 / 42 – / 15 18 / 4 / 22 / 60 x 40 / 2400 [sketch marked A and B / 4¼ by 6 5 / 8 x 8 / 74   49
=   1200   74
                                       3600   20   196
                                                                                                                       343
                                                                                                                     3626

In lower margin at left: Base Line here – – – / [vertical arrow].

In lower margin at right: [sketch marked 'triangle'] Lonely tower [illegible] / Bellman 9 / Remember the nearest ox to be light the next behind the [illegible].

No. XXI(d) is inscribed in top margin in the artist's hand: [Illegible] supper under arbour / [illegible]/ [illegible] half [illegible] very deep & very silvery.

In bottom margin at left: This is a third each way / of Miltons [illegible].

In the bottom margin at right: Darkest ox / just above that – then with shadowed mass of hedge / will enforce half-tint of buildings / Mind lit midd. T & its sense of colour.

In right-hand margin: extreme dark / Cologne / nearly bistre / Ground of trees Raw sie[nna] / length of Club Plate / 10 by 7½ / Chapter / Romans 11 / V12 & [illegible] / of Ch 5.

There is also an illegible inscription in the left-hand margin. Most of the inscriptions are much rubbed or faded and may be read only with difficulty. The reference to Romans is presumably to Paul's Epistle to the Romans, but there is little or nothing of relevance to this work either in Chapter 11, v.12 or in Chapter 5.

XXII   THE LONELY TOWER: Etching and related paintings

   One of two etchings completed for Milton's poems

   XXII(a) State 2 (before 1879). Plate size: 189 x 252 mm; etched surface: 165 to 167 x 233 mm. Retouched with pencil, chalk and wash.
   Signed in lower left-hand corner of plate: Saml. Palmer.
   Inscribed in Samuel Palmer's hand: For Touching [space] 3rd P/5—Canvas [space] think of Angle.
   In another hand, probably A. H. Palmer's: Private Press.
   On verso: Marden Ash Gilbert.
   Victoria and Albert Museum (ref. no. E457-1953)

   XXII(b) State 5.
   Signed in pencil: Samuel Palmer.
   Inscribed in bottom margin in A. H. Palmer's hand: AHP Private Press / Trial Proof.
   Victoria and Albert Museum (ref. no. E1895-1919)

   XXII(c) The cancelled copperplate with modern restrikes taken from this (see below).
   David Gould, Esq.

   XXII(d) Wash-drawing, ?1864.
   Bistre ink, crayon with scraped highlights, charcoal and white chalk (1864). Sheet size: 260 x 354 mm; drawing size: 203 x 286 mm.
   Inscribed illegibly in right margin.
   Inscribed on reverse in A. H. Palmer's hand: The First design for the "Lonely Tower"

Milton Drawing. . Never Exhibited / See my note No. 145 in the Catalogue of the Victoria & Albert Museum / Exhibition page 51 as to the occasional discordent use of white. A.H.P.

Cincinnati Art Museum

XXII(e) Watercolour and gouache, 1868.
With thick gum in places, on London board mounted on wood panel. Size: 510 x 705 mm. Inscribed as below.

Yale Center for British Art, Paul Mellon Collection

XXII(f) Watercolour, ? after 1864.
Size: 165 x 235 mm. Squared in pencil.

Huntington Library and Art Gallery, San Marino, California   Reproduction shown

For the genesis of this etching, see above, p. 71 and correspondence referred to.

This etching is considered to be one of the most successful works of Palmer's later years. It was completed in 1879, though the exact date of its commencement is not known. Seven states of the etching are recorded.

The Cincinnati design, No. XXII(d), is squared and, as indicated by A. H. Palmer's inscription on the verso, was certainly used by Samuel Palmer as the working design for the much larger watercolour No. XXII(e). It was probably also used by Palmer in making the etching which is slightly smaller than this wash-drawing. The mood and mastery of technique in this design recall Palmer's earlier Shoreham work.

There are considerable changes in composition between the early design, the etching and the finished watercolour, which was done for Valpy, No. XXII(e). This watercolour, now belonging to the Yale Center for British Art, Paul Mellon Collection, was dated 1868 in Christie's catalogue of the sale of 18 June 1892. A label pasted on the back of the frame has the following inscription in the artist's hand:

No: 1

The Lonely Tower
Or let my lamp at midnight hour,
Be seen in some high lonely tower,
Where I may oft outwatch the Bear,
With thrice great Hermes.

Samuel Palmer

The modernized quotation is from *Il Penseroso* (lines 85-8), which the work illustrates. It is reproduced in *The Shorter Poems of John Milton*, where the composition has been reversed in error.

There is a further watercolour design belonging to the Huntington Art Gallery, California, No. XXII(f), which could not be shown in the Exhibition owing to the terms of its bequest. This watercolour, which is squared, is exactly the size of the etching and is very similar in composition. It is probably the final design for the etching. A monochrome reproduction of this is shown in the Exhibition.

The cancelled plate, No. XXII(c), has been skilfully restored, but traces of the cancelling can be discerned. The small pane marks, where it was knocked up from the back ready for restoration, are also visible, as is the stamp of the manufacturer, Jones and Kimber of London.

The plate was restored by Macbeth Raeburn at the Liverpool School of Art. Part of the foliage of the tree immediately above the moon has disappeared, leaving a roughly pentagonal space filled with horizontal lines. The shape of the moon is completely altered to a less well-defined and thinner crescent. Many of the horizontal lines in the sky in and around the moon have disappeared and been replaced by others, which are broken and lacking in definition. All but a few traces of the trilithons beneath the moon have disappeared. There are faint signs of cancelling lines as follows: horizontally, about 32 mm, up from the bottom edge, extending across the whole design; vertically, about 78 mm in from the right-hand edge and extending from the right-hand ankle of the nearer reclining figure, as far as the horizon under the moon; in some better-printed impressions these signs are difficult to see.

The recto of the copperplate itself is shown together with photographic reproductions of the recto and the verso of the plate. Also exhibited are two modern restrikes from the cancelled plate, showing both a wiped proof of the type approved by Samuel Palmer and a more heavily inked pull as in certain of the later published states, the printing of which was a great disappointment to him (see pp. 23 and 25).

The initial edition from the cancelled plate was made by C. H. Welch of Ivor Place, London. There were twenty impressions numbered I to XX. A further small edition and a number of trial proofs have also been made from the cancelled plate and are now dispersed. For the convenience of collectors it is hoped that exact details of these can be recorded in the forthcoming William Blake Trust publication: *The Complete Etchings of Samuel Palmer and his Illustrations for Virgil and Milton.*

XXIII   MORNING or THE DRIPPING EAVES   1869

> Watercolour and gouache on London board. Size: 502 x 708 mm.
> Signed bottom left-hand corner: S. PALMER. Inscribed as below.
> *The Trustees of the Chatsworth Settlement (Devonshire Collections)*

A label pasted on the back of the frame has the following inscription in the artist's hand:

No. 2, Samuel Palmer

Morn,
Not trickt and frounct, as she was wont
With the Attic Boy to hunt;
But kerchieft in a comely cloud,
While rocking winds are piping loud,
Or usher'd with a shower still
When the gust hath blown his fill,
Ending on the rustling leaves,
With minute drops from off the eaves.

The modernized quotation is from *Il Penseroso* (lines 123–30) which the work illustrates. The year 1869 is that given to the work in Christie's catalogue of the sale of 18 June 1892.

Compare the distant figure at the left with that in the background of 'In a Shoreham Garden' (shown in the Exhibition), and with the distant figure in the left background of 'The Dell of Comus'. The lighting of this section of the composition is like that in the oil and tempera 'Pastoral Scene' (1835; Ashmolean Museum) and the moonlit field in 'Cornfield by Moonlight, with the Evening Star' (about 1830), kindly loaned for the Exhibition by Lord Clark.

The mottled effect previously mentioned is in evidence, and the trees and cottage are of types already noticed.

XXIV(a)   THE WATERS MURMURING   Before 1877

> Chalk and wash. Sheet size: 273 x 381 mm; painted area: 203 x 282 mm.
> Inscribed as below.
> *Victoria and Albert Museum* (ref. no. E1320-1925)

This work is a study for the watercolour following.

Inscribed in the artist's hand; reading clockwise from top right-hand corner: . . . Foliage ? If so a particle of sky A / [arrow] / A / [arrow] This near Rock with great downward wipe of dark. [Drawing of branches and tree] sunglow / gilding / that part of dark under . . . [illegible] Head of figure about ⅜ inch lower ground on which . . . Tree Trunk getting darker downwards / away from the Golden influence [illegible] [A drawing of a figure bending forwards to left] [illegible] [illegible] Heather Hill.

XXIV(b)   THE WATERS MURMURING   1877

> Watercolour and gouache on London board. Size: 508 x 698 mm.
> Signed bottom left-hand corner: Samuel Palmer. Inscribed as below.
> *Mrs. Cecil Keith*

A label pasted on the back panel of the frame has the following inscription in the artist's hand:

No. 1. "The Water Murmuring"
From Il Penseroso
There in close covert by some brook,
Where no profaner eye may look,
Hide me from day's garish eye,
While the bee with honied thigh,
That at her flowery work doth sing,
And the waters murmuring
With such concert as they keep
Entice the dewy-feathered sleep
Samuel Palmer
Furze Hill, Mead Vale, Red Hill, Surrey

The modernized quotation is from *Il Penseroso* (lines 139-46) which the work illustrates. The year 1877 is that given to the work in Christie's catalogue of the sale of 18 June 1892.

The dancing figure in the left-hand background has affinities with those in 'A Towered City'. The distant hill is probably a memory of a Devonshire tor. The composition in general is related to that of 'The Dell of Comus'.

XXV(a)   THE BROTHERS IN COMUS LINGERING UNDER THE VINE
Before 1856

Sepia wash touched with white. Size: 175 x 238 mm.
Victoria and Albert Museum (ref. no. E1321-1925)

This study for the watercolour following, No. XXV(b), is one of Palmer's finest mixed-media designs, and is reminiscent of many of the Shoreham studies.

The mood of this work, with its distant sunburst, is closely related to that of the upper subject in the etching 'The Vine', while the boscage recalls that in the etching 'The Morning of Life'. The figures of the brothers, too, have fairly close parallels in the central figure and in that on the extreme right in 'The Vine'.

XXV(b)   THE BROTHERS IN COMUS LINGERING UNDER THE VINE
1856

Watercolour and gouache on London board mounted on wood panel (see below). Sight size: 537 x 749 mm.
Signed lower right-hand corner in backward-sloping capitals: S. PALMER. Inscribed as below.
Private collection

A label pasted on the back panel of the frame has the following inscription in the artist's hand:

> The Brothers in Comus
> Two such I saw, what time ye labour'd ox
> In his loose traces from the furrow came
> And the swink'd hedger at his supper sat;
> I saw them under a green mantling vine,
> That crawls along the side of yon small hill,
> Plucking ripe clusters from the tender shoots.
> Samuel Palmer

The modernized quotation is from *Comus* (lines 291-6) which the work illustrates.

The London board on which the work is painted is apparently laid down on a wood panel, but this could not be confirmed as it was not possible to remove it from the frame. The board is impressed with the name NEWMAN, and as Palmer bought materials from the artist's colourman of that name at 24 Soho Square, London, it was probably a prepared board.

XXVI THE DELL OF COMUS 1855

Watercolour and gouache on London board. Size: 540 x 749 mm.
The Royal Pavilion, Art Gallery and Museums, Brighton

The work illustrates the lines:

> This evening late by then the chewing flocks
> Had ta'n their supper on the savoury Herb
> Of Knot-grass dew-besprent, and were in fold,
> I sate me down to watch upon a bank
> With Ivy canopied, and interwove
> With flaunting Hony-suckle, and began
> Wrapt in a pleasing fit of melancholy
> To meditate my rural minstrelsie,
>
> *Comus*, lines 540-7

The poplar-like saplings, typical of many Shoreham drawings, are again evident here. Like each of the three *Comus* designs, the work has an enclosed almost womb-like mood, and in this, though the forms are different, resembles a number of works of the Shoreham period, for example 'The Skirts of a Wood' (1825; Ashmolean Museum), 'Coming from Evening Church' (1830; The Tate Gallery), and 'Full Moon and Deer' (about 1829-30; Victoria and Albert Museum).

The group of dancers at the right have details resembling those in Claude's *Liber Veritatis* drawing 'Landscape with the Adoration of the Golden Calf' (plate 129).

XXVII THE BROTHERS, GUIDED BY THE ATTENDANT SPIRIT, DISCOVER THE PALACE AND TOWERS OF COMUS 1856

Watercolour and gouache on London board mounted on wood panel. Size: 536 x 749 mm.
Signed lower right-hand corner in backward-sloping capitals: SAMUEL PALMER. Inscribed as below.
Private collection

A label pasted on the back panel of the frame has the following inscription in the artist's hand: The Brothers and the / attendant Spirit, approach /-ing the Palace of Comus.

> – With dauntless hardihood
> And brandish't blade rushing on him
> Samuel Palmer

The modernized quotation is from *Comus* (lines 650-51), which the work illustrates.

More than any other work in the Milton series, this is dominated by Palmer's memories of his visit to Italy in 1837-9. The Palace bears several similarities to the Villa d'Este and the cypresses in

77

front of it recall the famous specimens in the garden of that palace. Palmer made several studies both of the Villa and of the cypresses, and used both in 1846 in an illustration to *Pictures from Italy* by Charles Dickens.

The same remarks about the London board and wood panel apply here as to No. XXV(b).

RELATED PAINTINGS AND PORTRAITS OF SAMUEL PALMER

1 RUTH RETURNED FROM GLEANING *c.* 1828

Watercolour with pen and ink wash heightened with white; traces of pencil. Size: 29 x 394 mm.
(ref. no. E3449-1923)

Nos. *1-9* are in the Victoria and Albert Museum. Nos. *4-6* are in one mount; also Nos. *7* and *8*.

2 THE PRIMITIVE COTTAGE 1828–9

Pen and sepia ink, grey and sepia wash, heightened with white with traces of pencil on grey paper. Size: 224 x 302 mm.
(ref. no. E452-1953)

3 IN A SHOREHAM GARDEN 1829

Watercolour and gouache. Size: 279 x 222 mm.
(ref. no. P32-1926)

4 A KENTISH IDYL 1829–30

Sepia. Size: 86 x 106 mm.
(ref. no. E453-1953)

Landscape sketch: in the foreground dark trees, through which a bright light breaks.

5 A KENTISH IDYL *c.* 1833

Indian ink wash. Squared in pencil. Size: 149 x 176 mm.
(ref. no. E643-1920)

A hill rises above the trees to the right; shadowy distance is seen to the left.

6 COMPOSITION 1829–30

>Wash and body colour. Size: 135 x 94 mm.
>(ref. no. E644-1920)

In the background, trees, through the tops of which is seen the full moon; in the foreground, the figure of a woman and three deer.

7 A VILLAGE CHURCH AMONG TREES *c.* 1830

>Black and grey watercolour. Size: 184 x 151 mm.
>(ref. no. P33-1953)

8 A COUNTRY ROAD LEADING TOWARDS A CHURCH 1830

>Dark sepia on card. Size: 183 x 149 mm.
>(ref. no. P34-1953)

9 SAMUEL PALMER'S SKETCH-BOOK 1824

>Size: 187 x 115 mm.
>(ref. nos. E2359-1928 (back); E3514-1928 (front); E3513-1928 (front))

Three leaves on one mount.

10 'CORNFIELD BY MOONLIGHT, WITH THE EVENING STAR' *c.* 1830

>Watercolour, gouache and pen. Size: 197 x 298 mm.
>*Lord Clark*

11 THE SHEARERS 1833-4

>Oil and tempera. Size: 515 x 711 mm.
>*Private collection*

12 THE FORUM, ROME *c.* 1837–9

>Watercolour and gouache over pencil. Size: 311 x 416 mm.
>*Sir Trenchard Cox*

13 THE STREET OF THE TOMBS, POMPEII, BEFORE THE EXCAVATIONS 1838

>Watercolour and gouache. Size: 289 x 419 mm.
>*Victoria and Albert Museum* (ref. no. P28-1919)

14 THE VILLA D'ESTE 1838

> Watercolour and gouache. Size: 273 x 373 mm.
> *Victoria and Albert Museum* (ref. no. P29-1919)

According to the Victoria and Albert Museum catalogue, 1926: 'On the back of the backboard is pencilled "The Villa d'Este 1837 Samual Palmer panted [*sic*] from nature".' This cannot be checked as the drawing is now laid down. The date 1837 is an error as Palmer did not visit the Villa d'Este until 1838.

15 A FARM YARD NEAR PRINCES RISBOROUGH, BUCKS. 1846

> Watercolour. Size: 392 x 540 mm.
> Inscribed as below.
> *Victoria and Albert Museum* (ref. no. P23-1919)

Signed lower left: Samuel PALMER. SP monogram lower right.
  A label from the backboard of the frame, now separately preserved, is inscribed in the artist's hand: A Farm-yard / near Prince's Risborough / Bucks. / N.B. No picture either in oil or / water colours should be so / hung as to receive direct / sunlight during any part of / the day. S.P.
  A card behind the drawing, now apparently lost, was inscribed in the artist's hand: Entering the Farm Yard. Size of mount board to be ordered 27¾ x 21½.

16 TINTAGEL CASTLE, APPROACHING RAIN *c.* 1848

> Gouache over pencil. Size: 302 x 440 mm.
> *Ashmolean Museum*

17 LANDSCAPE WITH WINDMILL, FIGURES AND CATTLE
1851 or earlier

> Watercolour, heightened with chinese white; some scratching. Size: 537 x 756 mm.
> Signed lower right: S. PALMER.
> *Victoria and Albert Museum* (ref. no. 1204-1886)

This is probably a view near Pulborough, Sussex. A watercolour 'Summer Storm near Pulborough, Sussex' (Gallery of South Australia, Adelaide) appears to be a different view of the same subject.

18 WILMOT'S HILL, KENT *c.* 1851

> Watercolour and gouache with some pen and ink over pencil on buff or discoloured white paper. Size: 276 x 381 mm.
> Inscribed lower left side, partly obliterated and somewhat unclearly: [obliterated] cow belongs to left side.
> *Yale Center for British Art* (ref. no. 63/4/26/42)

Another version of this subject, probably a study for this drawing, was in the possession of P. and D. Colnaghi and Co. Ltd. in 1977.

This drawing was previously known incorrectly as Wimlett's (or Ormlett's) Hill.

19 STUDY OF WAVES 1855 or earlier

> Watercolour and gouache over pencil on buff-grey paper. Size: 146 x 225 mm.
> *Yale Center for British Art* (ref. no. B1975.4.664)

This is one of a series of similar subjects.

20 THE HERDSMAN *c.* 1855

> Watercolour and gouache. Size: 521 x 737 mm.
> *Borough Art Galleries, Oldham*

21 THE DAWN OF LIFE *c.* 1859

> Watercolour laid down on thick card. Size: 254 x 438 mm (cut down from an originally larger size).
> Inscribed on reverse in an unidentified hand: The Dawn of Life / Samuel Palmer / Glasgow International Art Exht. 1901 / lent by S. Bainbridge Esq. / Hatfield House / Lincoln. / From the [*end of inscription*].
> There are also two circled numbers: 13175 and 243.
> *Harris Museum and Art Gallery, Preston*

22 'GOING HOME AT CURFEW TIME' 1864

> Watercolour. Size: 279 x 403 mm.
> *Victoria and Albert Museum* (ref. no. 40-1892)

23 HOPE, OR THE LIFTING OF THE CLOUD 1865 or earlier

> Watercolour and gouache. Size: 260 x 375 mm.
> Signed lower right-hand corner: s. PALMER.
> *Private Collection*

Exhibited by the Old Water-Colour Society, winter, 1865 (348), with the quotation: 'The day at first was sombre, like the shadowy turrets we were to explore. Then there was a distant gleam; the breeze began to stir, and the rain-cloud slowly rising, disclosed the mountains.'

24 PAPIGNO ON THE NAR, BELOW THE FALLS OF TERNI 1871

> Watercolour and gouache on buff paper. Size: 511 x 702 mm.
> Signed, bottom right: S. PALMER.
> *Bolton Museum and Art Gallery*

Exhibited by the Old Water-Colour Society, winter, 1871 (378), with the quotation: 'Fluminaque antiquos subterlabentia muros.'

25 THE TRAVELLERS 1875 or earlier

> Watercolour, gouache, pen and ink and varnish over pencil, with surface scratching. Size: 268 x 444 mm.
> Signed lower left-hand corner: S. PALMER.
> *Whitworth Art Gallery, University of Manchester*

26 MOUNTAIN STREAMS AND AN ANCIENT FORTRESS 1879

> Watercolour. Painted area: 148 x 200 mm; sheet size: 169 x 257 mm.
> *Victoria and Albert Museum* (ref. no. P33-1919)

PORTRAITS OF SAMUEL PALMER

27 Samuel Palmer aged 14 by Henry Walter 1819

> Pencil. Size: 222 x 192 mm.
> Signed: H. Walter, July 20. 1819.
> *British Museum*

28 Self-Portrait of Samuel Palmer, aged about 19 *c.* 1824

> Black chalk, heightened with white, on buff paper. Size: 291 x 229 mm.
> *Ashmolean Museum*

29 Caricature of Palmer, aged about 20 by George Richmond 1825

> Pencil. Size: 155 x 108 mm.
> Inscribed: Sambo Palmer Sep 22 1825 [or possibly 1829, in which case he is 24].
> *Victoria and Albert Museum* (ref. no. 1299-1925)

Palmer is seen from the back, wearing a very wide-brimmed hat and carrying a large umbrella upside down.

30 Palmer, head and shoulders, aged about 23   by George Richmond   *c.* 1828

Sepia ink sketch. Sheet size: 191 x 295 mm; image size: 95 x 60 mm.
Inscribed in pencil: Portrait of Samuel Palmer probably by Mr Richmond [and on the back] Qy use for the proposed life of SP and For Sir Frank Short.
Victoria and Albert Museum (ref. no. E458-1953)

31 Samuel Palmer assuming a character   by George Richmond   *c.* 1828

Pen and brown ink over black chalk on grey paper. Size: 151 x 121 mm.
Signed lower right: GR [and below] 1828 [possibly 1825].
Inscribed centre: SP as Mr. Richardson (?) in Dundas. [lower centre] S. Palmer assuming a character.
Yale Center for British Art, Paul Mellon Collection Reproduction Shown (ref. no. B1975.4.675)

32 Half-Length portrait of Samuel Palmer   by George Richmond   *c.* 1829

Pencil and gouache. Size: 231 x 187 mm.
Victoria and Albert Museum (ref. no. E1298-1925)

33 Drawing of Samuel Palmer's Head   by John Linnell   ?1829

Pencil on buff paper. Paper size: 198 x 285 mm; image size: 165 x 152 mm.
Inscribed at top right: Study for Emmaus Group [at bottom] J. Linnell from S. Palmer's Head.
Mrs. J. L. Burton

Palmer served as a model for the figure on Christ's left in 'The Journey to Emmaus' by John Linnell.

34 Samuel Palmer   by George Richmond   1829

Miniature, watercolour and gouache on ivory. Size: 83 x 70 mm.
Inscribed on the card on which the miniature is mounted, probably in the artist's hand: Saml Palmer Esq. (Painter) / Painted by Geo Richmond in Half Moon St in Novr. 1829 / 129 / Exhibited at Rl Acy. 1830.
Incised on the metal back of the frame, probably in the artist's hand: Saml Palmer E / 1829 / Painted by / exhibited 1830 / Geo Richmond / in 1829 / TKR GR / 1874
National Portrait Gallery

35 Portrait of Samuel Palmer   by Henry Walter   1835

Watercolour and pen. Size: 541 x 362 mm.
Described in George Richmond's hand vertically at lower left: Henry Walter died and was buried at Torquay / April 23, 1849. Though he left but few works they are / all marked by high artistic qualities and fine sentiment. / Mr Walter was about 63 when he died. Horizontally at bottom left: This fine drawing and admirable likeness of / Samuel Palmer (Painter) by his friend Henry Walter I give to the Print Room of the British Museum. / Palmer died at Reigate May 24, 1881: He was about 74. [signed] George Richmond, R.A., 1883.

CHRONOLOGY

1805 Born in London, 27 January.

1819 Sells his first picture, 'Landscape', exhibited at the British Institution.

1822 Meets John Linnell in September.

1823 Meets George Richmond.

1824 Introduced to William Blake by Linnell.

1826 Meets Edward Calvert. Moves to Shoreham in Kent, with his father.

1832 Buys a London house, 4 Grove Street, Lisson Grove, but continues until his marriage to spend time at Shoreham.

1833 Falls in love with Hannah, Linnell's eldest daughter. Visits Devon.

1835 Visits Devon, Somerset and Wales.

1837 Marries Hannah Linnell on 30 September.
Visits Italy for two years with Hannah, accompanied during part of the time by Mr. and Mrs. George Richmond.

1839 They settle at Grove Street on their return.

1842 Birth of his son, Thomas More, 27 January. Visits Thatcham in Berkshire.

1843 Elected an Associate of the Society of Painters in Water-Colours.

1844 Birth of his daughter, Mary Elizabeth. Visits Guildford and Wales.

1845 Visits Princes Risborough, Buckinghamshire.

1846 Illustrates *Pictures from Italy* for Dickens.

1847 Death of Mary Elizabeth Palmer, 15 December.

1848 Moves to 1A Victoria Road, Kensington. Visits Cornwall and Devon.

1849 Visits Devon.

1850 Elected a member of the Etching Club. Publication of his first four etchings, 'The Willow', 'The Skylark', 'Sunset' and 'Christmas'.

1851 Moves to 6 Douro Place, Kensington.

1852 Publication of etching 'The Vine'.

1853 Birth of his son, Alfred Herbert, 25 September.

1854 Elected a member of the Society of Painters in Water-Colours.

1855 Approached for recollections by Alexander Gilchrist, William Blake's biographer. Completes the watercolour 'The Dell of Comus' from Milton's *Comus*.

1856 At about this time begins to translate Virgil's *Eclogues* into English. Completes watercolours, 'The Brothers in Comus lingering under the Vine' and 'The Brothers discover The Palace of Comus' from Milton's *Comus*.

1857 Publication of etchings 'The Sleeping Shepherd' and 'The Rising Moon'.

1858 Visits Cornwall and Devon with Thomas More.

1861 Takes family for a visit to Abinger in Surrey. Thomas More dies there, 11 July. Takes up residence at Redhill, first at Elm Cottage, afterwards at Park Lane. Completion of etchings 'The Early Ploughman' and 'The Morning of Life' at about this time.

1862 Takes up residence at Furze Hill House, Mead Vale, Redhill, where he lived for the remainder of his life.

1863 Sells a picture, 'Twilight: the Chapel by the Bridge' to John Ruskin's solicitor, Leonard Rowe Valpy, at the winter exhibition of the Water-Colour Society.

1864 Valpy commissions the large watercolours illustrating *Il Penseroso* and *L'Allegro*.

1868 Completes watercolours 'A Towered City' (*L'Allegro*) and 'The Lonely Tower' (*Il Penseroso*).

1869 Completes watercolour 'Morning' (*Il Penseroso*).

1870 Completes watercolour 'The Curfew' (*Il Penseroso*).

1872 On the advice of the art critic, Philip Gilbert Hamerton, plans to illustrate his translation of Virgil.

1873 Completes watercolour illustrating Milton's 'Lycidas.'.

1877 Completes watercolour 'The Waters Murmuring' *(Il Penseroso)*.

1879 Completion of etchings 'The Bellman' and 'The Lonely Tower'.

1880 Completion of etching 'Opening the Fold'.

1881 Work partly completed on four etchings for Virgil's *Eclogues*: 'The Homeward Star', 'The Cypress Grove', 'The Sepulchre' and 'Moeris and Galatea'. Completes watercolours 'The Eastern Gate' (*L'Allegro*), and 'The Bellman' (*Il Penseroso*); 'The Prospect' (ibid.) remains uncompleted. Dies 24 May.

SELECTED BIBLIOGRAPHY

ALEXANDER, R. G. *A Catalogue of the Etchings of Samuel Palmer*. Publication No. 16 of the Print Collectors' Club. London, 1937.

ARTS COUNCIL. *Samuel Palmer and his Circle. The Shoreham Period*. Arts Council of Great Britain, London, 1957.

ASHMOLEAN MUSEUM. *Paintings and Drawings by Samuel Palmer*. Ashmolean Museum, Oxford, n.d.

BINYON, Laurence. *The Followers of William Blake*. Halton and Truscott Smith, London, 1925.

CALVERT, Samuel. *A Memoir of Edward Calvert Artist by his Third Son*. Sampson Low, Marston and Co., London, 1893.

CECIL, David. *Visionary and Dreamer Two Poetic Painters: Samuel Palmer and Edward Burne-Jones*. Constable and Co., London, 1966; Princeton University Press, Princeton, N.J., 1969. The American edition is more lavishly illustrated.

FABER GALLERY. *Samuel Palmer*. Faber and Faber, London, n.d.

FINCH, Mrs. Eliza. *Memorials of the Late Francis Oliver Finch*. Longman, Green, Longman, Roberts and Green, London, 1865.

GILCHRIST, Alexander. *Life of William Blake*. Everyman's Library, London, 1942. There are several earlier editions.

GLEESON, Larry (Editor). *Followers of Blake*. Santa Barbara Museum of Art, 1976.

GRIGSON, Geoffrey. *Samuel Palmer the Visionary Years*. Kegan Paul, London, 1947.

—— *Samuel Palmer's Valley of Vision*. Phoenix House, London, 1960.

HAMERTON, Philip Gilbert. *Etching and Etchers*. Macmillan & Co., London, 1868. Other editions were issued in 1876 and 1880.

HARDIE, Martin. 'The Etched Work of Samuel Palmer', *Print Collector's Quarterly*, vol. 3, pp. 207-40, Boston, Mass., 1913.

—— 'Samuel Palmer', *The Old Water-Colour Society's Club Fourth Annual Volume*. Edited by Randall Davies, London, 1927.

—— *Samuel Palmer*. Publication No. 7 of the Print Collectors' Club. London, 1928.

—— *Water-colour Painting in Britain. II The Romantic Period.* Edited by Dudley Snelgrove with Jonathan Mayne and Basil Taylor; B.T. Batsford Ltd., London, 1967.

LISTER, Raymond. *Beulah to Byzantium: a Study of Parallels in the Works of W. B. Yeats, William Blake, Samuel Palmer and Edward Calvert.* Dolmen Press, Dublin, 1965.

—— *The Complete Etchings of Samuel Palmer and The Related Illustrations for Virgil and Milton.* Trianon Press for the William Blake Trust, London, 1979.

—— *Edward Calvert.* G. Bell and Son, London, 1962.

—— *Samuel Palmer a Biography.* Faber and Faber, London, 1974.

—— *Samuel Palmer and his Etchings.* Faber and Faber, London, 1969.

—— 'Samuel Palmer's Milton Watercolours', in *The Connoisseur*, London, January, 1977.

—— *Samuel Palmer in Palmer Country.* East Bergholt, 1978.

MacCOLL, D. S. *Nineteenth Century Art.* Glasgow, 1902.

MALINS, Edward. *Samuel Palmer's Italian Honeymoon.* Oxford University Press, London, 1968.

MATHER, Frank Jewett, Junr. 'Samuel Palmer's Virgil Etchings', *Print Collector's Quarterly*, vol. 24, No. 3, pp. 253-64, Kansas City, 1937.

PALMER, A. H. *The Life and Letters of Samuel Palmer Painter and Etcher.* Seeley and Co., London, 1892. Reprinted with an Introductory Essay by Raymond Lister and a Preface by Kathleen Raine; Eric and Joan Stevens, London, 1972.

—— *Samuel Palmer a Memoir.* Seeley and Co., London, 1882.

PALMER, Samuel. *The Eclogues of Virgil. An English Version.* Seeley and Co., London, 1883.

—— *The Letters of Samuel Palmer.* Edited by Raymond Lister, 2 vols., Clarendon Press, Oxford, 1974.

—— *Samuel Palmer's Sketch-Book 1824.* Facsimile with an Introduction and Commentary by Martin Butlin; Trianon Press for the William Blake Trust, London, 1962.

—— *The Shorter Poems of John Milton with Twelve Illustrations by Samuel Palmer.* London, 1889.

PRESSLY, William L., Junr. 'Samuel Palmer: the Etching Dream', *Record of the Art Museum Princeton University*, vol. XXIX, no. 2, 1970.

—— 'Samuel Palmer and the Pastoral Convention', ibid., vol. XXVIII, no. 2, 1969.

RAY, Gordon N. *The Illustrator and the Book in England from 1790 to 1914.* Oxford, 1976.

REDGRAVE, Samuel & Richard. *A Century of Painters.* Edited by R. Todd, London, 1947.

VICTORIA AND ALBERT MUSEUM. *Catalogue of an Exhibition of Drawings, Etchings and Woodcuts by Samuel Palmer and other Disciples of William Blake.* Victoria and Albert Museum, London, 1926.